William the Conqueror

by E. A. Freeman

William the Conqueror, by E. A. Freeman

William the Conqueror

Contents
Introduction
The Early Years of William
William's First Visit to England
The Reign of William in Normandy
Harold's Oat to William
The Negotiations of Duke William
William's Invasion of England
The Conquest of England
The Settlement of England
The Revolts against William
The Last Years of William

CHAPTER I—INTRODUCTION

The history of England, like the land and its people, has been specially insular, and yet no land has undergone deeper influences from without. No land has owed more than England to the personal action of men not of native birth. Britain was truly called another world, in opposition to the world of the European mainland, the world of Rome. In every age the history of Britain is the history of an island, of an island great enough to form a world of itself. In speaking of Celts or Teutons in Britain, we are speaking, not simply of Celts and Teutons, but of Celts and Teutons parted from their kinsfolk on the mainland, and brought under the common influences of an island world. The land has seen several settlements from outside, but the settlers have always been brought under the spell of their insular position. Whenever settlement has not meant displacement, the new comers have been assimilated by the existing people of the land. When it has meant displacement, they have still become islanders, marked off from those whom they left behind by characteristics which were the direct result of settlement in an island world.

The history of Britain then, and specially the history of England, has been largely a history of elements absorbed and assimilated from without. But each of those elements has done somewhat to modify the mass into which it was absorbed. The English land and nation are not as they might have been if they had never in later times absorbed the Fleming, the French Huguenot, the German Palatine. Still less are they as they might have been, if they had not in earlier times absorbed the greater elements of the Dane and the Norman. Both were assimilated; but both modified the character and destiny of the people into whose substance they were absorbed. The conquerors from Normandy were silently and peacefully lost in the greater mass of the English people; still we can never be as if the Norman had never come among us. We ever bear about us the signs of his presence. Our colonists have carried those signs with them into distant lands, to remind men that settlers in America and Australia came from a land which the Norman once entered as a conqueror. But that those signs of his presence hold the place which they do hold in our mixed political being, that, badges of conquest as they are, no one feels them to be badges of conquest—all this comes of the fact that, if the Norman came as a conqueror, he came as a conqueror of a special, perhaps almost of an unique kind. The Norman Conquest of England has, in its nature and in its results, no exact parallel in history. And that it has no exact parallel in history is largely owing to the character and position of the man who wrought it. That the history of England for the last eight hundred years has been what it has been has largely come of the personal character of a single man. That we are what we are to this day largely comes of the fact that there was a moment when our national destiny might be said to hang on the will of a single man, and that that man was William, surnamed at different stages of his life and memory, the Bastard, the Conqueror, and the Great.

With perfect fitness then does William the Norman, William the Norman Conqueror of England, take his place in a series of English statesmen. That so it should be is characteristic of English history. Our history has been largely wrought for us by men who have come in from without, sometimes as conquerors, sometimes as the opposite of conquerors; but in whatever character they came, they had to put on the character of Englishmen, and to make their work an English work. From whatever land they came, on whatever mission they came, as statesmen they were English. William, the greatest of his class, is still but a member of a class. Along with him we must reckon a crowd of kings, bishops, and high officials in many ages of our history. Theodore of Tarsus and Cnut of Denmark, Lanfranc of Pavia and Anselm of Aosta, Randolf Flambard and Roger of Salisbury, Henry of Anjou and Simon of Montfort, are all written on a list of which William is but the foremost. The largest number come in William's own generation and in the generations just before and after it. But the breed of England's adopted children and rulers never died out. The name of William the Deliverer stands, if not beside that of his namesake the Conqueror, yet surely alongside of the lawgiver from Anjou. And we count among the later worthies of England not a few men sprung from other lands, who did and are doing their work among us, and who, as statesmen at least, must count as English. As we look along the whole line, even among the conquering kings and their immediate instruments, their work never takes the shape of the rooting up of the earlier institutions of the land. Those institutions are modified, sometimes silently by the mere growth of events, sometimes formally and of set purpose. Old institutions get new names; new institutions are set up alongside of them. But the old ones are never swept away; they sometimes die out; they are never abolished. This comes largely of the absorbing and assimilating power of the island world. But it comes no less of personal character and personal circumstances, and pre-eminently of the personal character of the Norman Conqueror and of the circumstances in which he found himself.

Our special business now is with the personal acts and character of William, and above all with his acts and character as an English statesman. But the English reign of William followed on his earlier Norman reign, and its character was largely the result of his earlier Norman reign. A man of the highest natural gifts, he had gone through such a schooling from his childhood upwards as falls to the lot of few princes. Before he undertook the conquest of England, he had in some sort to work the conquest of Normandy. Of the ordinary work of a sovereign in a warlike age, the defence of his own land, the annexation of other lands, William had his full share. With the land of his overlord he had dealings of the most opposite kinds. He had to call in the help of the French king to put down rebellion in the Norman duchy, and he had to drive back more than one invasion of the French king at the head of an united Norman people. He added Domfront and Maine to his dominions, and the conquest of Maine, the work as much of statesmanship as of warfare, was the rehearsal of the conquest of England. There, under circumstances strangely like those of England, he learned his trade as conqueror, he learned to practise on a narrower field the same arts which he afterwards practised on a wider. But after all, William's own duchy was his special school; it was his life in his own duchy which specially helped to make him what he was. Surrounded by trials and difficulties almost from his cradle, he early learned the art of enduring trials and overcoming difficulties; he learned how to deal with men; he learned when to smite and when to spare; and it is not a little to his honour that, in the long course of such a reign as his, he almost always showed himself far more ready to spare than to smite.

Before then we can look at William as an English statesman, we must first look on him in the land in which he learned the art of statesmanship. We must see how one who started with all the disadvantages which are implied in his earlier surname of the Bastard came to win and to deserve his later surnames of the Conqueror and the Great.

CHAPTER II—THE EARLY YEARS OF WILLIAM—A.D. 1028-1051

If William's early reign in Normandy was his time of schooling for his later reign in England, his school was a stern one, and his schooling began early. His nominal reign began at the age of seven years, and his personal influence on events began long before he had reached the usual years of discretion. And the events of his minority might well harden him, while they could not corrupt him in the way in which so many princes have been corrupted. His whole position, political and personal, could not fail to have its effect in forming the man. He was Duke of the Normans, sixth in succession from Rolf, the founder of the Norman state. At the time of his accession, rather more than a hundred and ten years had passed since plunderers, occasionally settlers, from Scandinavia, had changed into acknowledged members of the Western or Karolingian kingdom. The Northmen, changed, name and thing, into *Normans*, were now in all things members of the Christian and French-speaking world. But French as the Normans of William's day had become, their relation to the kings and people of France was not a friendly one. At the time of the settlement of Rolf, the western kingdom of the Franks had not yet finally passed to the *Duces Francorum* at Paris; Rolf became the man of the Karolingian king at Laon. France and Normandy were two great duchies, each owning a precarious supremacy in the king of the West-Franks. On the one hand, Normandy had been called into being by a frightful dismemberment of the French duchy, from which the original Norman settlement had been cut off. France had lost in Rouen one of her greatest cities, and she was cut off from the sea and from the lower course of her own river. On the other hand, the French and the Norman dukes had found their interest in a close alliance; Norman support had done much to transfer the crown from Laon to Paris, and to make the *Dux Francorum* and the *Rex Francorum* the same person. It was the adoption of the French speech and manners by the Normans, and their steady alliance with the French dukes, which finally determined that the ruling element in Gaul should be Romance and not Teutonic, and that, of its Romance elements, it should be French and not Aquitanian. If the creation of Normandy had done much to weaken France as a duchy, it had done not a little towards the making of France as a kingdom. Laon and its crown, the undefined influence that went with the crown, the prospect of future advance to the south, had been bought by the loss of Rouen and of the mouth of the Seine.

There was much therefore at the time of William's accession to keep the French kings and the Norman dukes on friendly terms. The old alliance had been strengthened by recent good offices. The reigning king, Henry the First, owed his crown to the help of William's father Robert. On the other hand, the original ground of the alliance, mutual support against the Karolingian king, had passed away. A King of the French reigning at Paris was more likely to remember what the Normans had cost him as duke than what they had done for him as king. And the alliance was only an alliance of princes. The mutual dislike between the people of the two countries was strong. The Normans had learned French ways, but French and Normans had not become countrymen. And, as the fame of Normandy grew, jealousy was doubtless mingled with dislike. William, in short, inherited a very doubtful and dangerous state of relations towards the king who was at once his chief neighbour and his overlord.

More doubtful and dangerous still were the relations which the young duke inherited towards the people of his own duchy and the kinsfolk of his own house. William was not as yet the Great or the Conqueror, but he was the Bastard from the beginning. There was then no generally received doctrine as to the succession to kingdoms and duchies. Everywhere a single kingly or princely house supplied, as a rule, candidates for the succession. Everywhere, even where the elective doctrine was strong, a full-grown son was always likely to succeed his father. The growth of feudal notions too had greatly strengthened the hereditary principle. Still no rule had anywhere been laid down for cases where the late prince had not left a full-grown son. The question as to legitimate birth was equally unsettled. Irregular unions of all kinds, though condemned by the Church, were tolerated in practice, and were nowhere more common than among the Norman dukes. In truth the feeling of the kingliness of the stock, the doctrine that the king should be the son of a king, is better satisfied by the succession of the late king's bastard son than by sending for some distant kinsman, claiming perhaps only through females. Still bastardy, if it was often convenient to forget it, could always be turned against a man. The succession of a bastard was never likely to be quite undisputed or his reign to be quite undisturbed.

Now William succeeded to his duchy under the double disadvantage of being at once bastard and minor. He was born at Falaise in 1027 or 1028, being the son of Robert, afterwards duke, but then only Count of Hiesmois, by Herleva, commonly called Arletta, the daughter of Fulbert the tanner. There was no pretence of marriage between his parents; yet his father, when he designed William to succeed him, might have made him legitimate, as some of his predecessors had been made, by a marriage with his mother. In 1028 Robert succeeded his brother Richard in the duchy. In 1034 or 1035 he determined to go on pilgrimage to Jerusalem. He called on his barons to swear allegiance to his bastard of seven years old as his successor in case he never came back. Their wise counsel to stay at home, to look after his dominions and to raise up lawful heirs, was unheeded. Robert carried his point. The succession of young William was accepted by the Norman nobles, and was confirmed by the overlord Henry King of the French. The arrangement soon took effect. Robert died on his way back before the year 1035 was out, and his son began, in name at least, his reign of fifty-two years over the Norman duchy.

The succession of one who was at once bastard and minor could happen only when no one else had a distinctly better claim William could never have held his ground for a moment against a brother of his father of full age and undoubted legitimacy. But among the living descendants of former dukes some were themselves of doubtful legitimacy, some were shut out by their profession as churchmen, some claimed only through females. Robert had indeed two half-brothers, but they were young and their legitimacy was disputed; he had an uncle, Robert Archbishop of Rouen, who had been legitimated by the later marriage of his parents. The rival who in the end gave William most trouble was his cousin Guy of Burgundy, son of a daughter of his grandfather Richard the Good. Though William's succession was not liked, no one of these candidates was generally preferred to him. He therefore succeeded; but the first twelve years of his reign were spent in the revolts and conspiracies of unruly nobles, who hated the young duke as the one representative of law and order, and who were not eager to set any one in his place who might be better able to enforce them.

Nobility, so variously defined in different lands, in Normandy took in two classes of men. All were noble who had any kindred or affinity, legitimate or otherwise, with the ducal house. The natural children of Richard the Fearless were legitimated by his marriage with their mother Gunnor, and many of the great houses of Normandy sprang from her brothers and sisters. The mother of William received no such exaltation as this. Besides her son, she had borne to Robert a daughter Adelaide, and, after Robert's death, she married a Norman knight named Herlwin of Conteville. To him, besides a daughter, she bore two sons, Ode and Robert. They rose to high posts in Church and State, and played an important part in their half-brother's history. Besides men whose nobility was of this kind, there were also Norman houses whose privileges were older than the amours or marriages of any duke, houses whose greatness was as old as the settlement of Rolf, as old that is as the ducal power itself. The great men of both these classes were alike hard to control. A Norman baron of this age was well employed when he was merely rebelling against his prince or waging private war against a fellow baron. What specially marks the time is the frequency of treacherous murders wrought by men of the highest rank, often on harmless neighbours or unsuspecting guests. But victims were also found among those guardians of the young duke whose faithful discharge of their duties shows that the Norman nobility was not wholly corrupt. One indeed was a foreign prince, Alan Count of the Bretons, a grandson of Richard the Fearless through a daughter. Two others, the seneschal Osbern and Gilbert Count of Eu, were irregular kinsmen of the duke. All these were murdered, the Breton count by poison. Such a childhood as this made William play the man while he was still a child. The helpless boy had to seek for support of some kind. He got together the chief men of his duchy, and took a new guardian by their advice. But it marks the state of things that the new guardian was one of the murderers of those whom he succeeded. This was Ralph of Wacey, son of William's great-uncle, Archbishop Robert. Murderer as he was, he seems to have discharged his duty faithfully. There are men who are careless of general moral obligations, but who will strictly carry out any charge which appeals to personal honour. Anyhow Ralph's guardianship brought with it a certain amount of calm. But men, high in the young duke's favour, were still plotting against him, and they presently began to plot, not only against their prince but against their country. The disaffected nobles of Normandy sought for a helper against young William in his lord King Henry of Paris.

The art of diplomacy had never altogether slumbered since much earlier times. The king who owed his crown to William's father, and who could have no ground of offence against William himself, easily unnatural in the King of the French to wish to win back a sea-board which had been given up more than a hundred years before to an alien power, even though that power had, for much more than half of that time, acted more than a friendly part towards France. It was not unnatural that the French people should cherish a strong national dislike to the Normans and a strong wish that Rouen should again be a French city. But such motives were not openly avowed then any more than now. The alleged ground was quite different. The counts of Chartres were troublesome neighbours to the duchy, and the castle of Tillières had been built as a defence against them. An advance of the King's dominions had made Tillières a neighbour of France, and, as a neighbour, it was said to be a standing menace. The King of the French, acting in concert with the disaffected party in Normandy, was a dangerous enemy, and the young Duke and his counsellors determined to give up Tillières. Now comes the first distinct exercise of William's personal will. We are without exact dates, but the time can be hardly later than 1040, when William was from twelve to thirteen years old. At his special request, the defender of Tillières, Gilbert Crispin, who at first held out against French and Normans alike, gave up the castle to Henry. The castle was burned; the King promised not to repair it for four years. Yet he is said to have entered Normandy, to have laid waste William's native district of Hiesmois, to have supplied a French garrison to a Norman rebel named Thurstan, who held the castle of Falaise against the Duke, and to have ended by restoring Tillières as a menace against Normandy. And now the boy whose destiny had made him so early a leader of men had to bear his first arms against the fortress which looked down on his birth-place. Thurstan surrendered and went into banishment. William could set down his own Falaise as the first of a long list of towns and castles which he knew how to win without shedding of blood.

When we next see William's distinct personal action, he is still young, but no longer a child or even a boy. At nineteen or thereabouts he is a wise and valiant man, and his valour and wisdom are tried to the uttermost. A few years of comparative quiet were chiefly occupied, as a quiet time in those days commonly was, with ecclesiastical affairs. One of these specially illustrates the state of things with which William had to deal. In 1042, when the Duke was about fourteen, Normandy adopted the Truce of God in its later shape. It no longer attempted to establish universal peace; it satisfied itself with forbidding, under the strongest ecclesiastical censures, all private war and violence of any kind on certain days of the week. Legislation of this kind has two sides. It was an immediate gain if peace was really enforced for four days in the week; but that which was not forbidden on the other three could no longer be denounced as in itself evil. We are told that in no land was the Truce more strictly observed than in Normandy. But we may be sure that, when William was in the fulness of his power, the stern weight of the ducal arm was exerted to enforce peace on Mondays and Tuesdays as well as on Thursdays and Fridays.

It was in the year 1047 that William's authority was most dangerously threatened and that he was first called on to show in all their fulness the powers that were in him. He who was to be conqueror of Maine and conqueror of England was first to be conqueror of his own duchy. The revolt of a large part of the country, contrasted with the firm loyalty of another part, throws a most instructive light on the internal state of the duchy. There was, as there still is, a line of severance between the districts which formed the first grant to Rolf and those which were afterwards added. In these last a lingering remnant of old Teutonic life had been called into fresh strength by new settlements from Scandinavia. At the beginning of the reign of Richard the Fearless, Rouen, the French-speaking city, is emphatically contrasted with Bayeux, the once Saxon city and land, now the headquarters of the Danish speech. At that stage the Danish party was distinctly a heathen party. We are not told whether Danish was still spoken so late as the time of William's youth. We can hardly believe that the Scandinavian gods still kept any avowed worshippers. But the geographical limits of the revolt exactly fall in with the boundary which had once divided French and Danish speech, Christian and heathen worship. There was a wide difference in feeling on the two sides of the Dive. The older Norman settlements, now thoroughly French in tongue and manners, stuck faithfully to the Duke; the lands to the west rose against him. Rouen and Evreux were firmly loyal to William; Saxon Bayeux and Danish Coutances were the headquarters of his enemies.

When the geographical division took this shape, we are surprised at the candidate for the duchy who was put forward by the rebels. William was a Norman born and bred; his rival was in every sense a Frenchman. This was William's cousin Guy of Burgundy, whose connexion with the ducal house was only by the spindle-side. But his descent was of uncontested legitimacy, which gave him an excuse for claiming the duchy in opposition to the bastard grandson of the tanner. By William he had been enriched with great possessions, among which was the island fortress of Brionne in the Risle. The real object of the revolt was the partition of the duchy. William was to be dispossessed; Guy was to be duke in the lands east of Dive; the great lords of Western Normandy were to be left independent. To this end the lords of the Bessin and the Côtentin revolted, their leader being Neal, Viscount of Saint-Sauveur in the Côtentin. We are told that the mass of the people everywhere wished well to their duke; in the common sovereign lay their only chance of protection against their immediate lords. But the lords had armed force of the land at their bidding. They first tried to slay or seize the Duke himself, who chanced to be in the midst of them at Valognes. He escaped; we hear a stirring tale of his headlong ride from Valognes to Falaise. Safe among his own people, he planned his course of action. He first sought help of the man who could give him most help, but who had most wronged him. He went into France; he saw King Henry at Poissy, and the King engaged to bring a French force to William's help under his own command.

This time Henry kept his promise. The dismemberment of Normandy might have been profitable to France by weakening the power which had become so special an object of French jealousy; but with a king the common interest of princes against rebellious barons came first. Henry came with a French army, and fought well for his ally on the field of Val-ès-dunes. Now came the Conqueror's first battle, a tourney of horsemen on an open table-land just within the land of the rebels between Caen and Mezidon. The young duke fought well and manfully; but the Norman writers allow that it was French help that gained him the victory. Yet one of the many anecdotes of the battle points to a source of strength which was always ready to tell for any lord against rebellious vassals. One of the leaders of the revolt, Ralph of Tesson, struck with remorse and stirred by the prayers of his knights, joined the Duke just before the battle. He had sworn to smite William wherever he found him, and he fulfilled his oath by giving the Duke a harmless blow with his glove. How far an oath to do an unlawful act is binding is a question which came up again at another stage of William's life.

The victory at Val-ès-dunes was decisive, and the French King, whose help had done so much to win it, left William to follow it up. He met with but little resistance except at the stronghold of Brionne. Guy himself vanishes from Norman history. William had now conquered his own duchy, and conquered it by foreign help. For the rest of his Norman reign he had often to strive with enemies at home, but he had never to put down such a rebellion again as that of the lords of western Normandy. That western Normandy, the truest Normandy, had to yield to the more thoroughly Romanized lands to the east. The difference between them never again takes a political shape. William was now lord of all Normandy, and able to put down all later disturbers of the peace. His real reign now begins; from the age of nineteen or twenty, his acts are his own. According to his abiding practice, he showed himself a merciful conqueror. Through his whole reign he shows a distinct unwillingness to take human life except in fair fighting on the battle-field. No blood was shed after the victory of Val-ès-dunes; one rebel died in bonds; the others underwent no harder punishment than payment of fines, giving of hostages, and destruction of their castles. These castles were not as yet the vast and elaborate structures which arose in after days. A single strong square tower, or even a defence of wood on a steep mound surrounded by a ditch, was enough to make its owner dangerous. The possession of these strongholds made every baron able at once to defy his prince and to make himself a scourge to his neighbours. Every season of anarchy is marked by the building of castles; every return of order brings with it their overthrow as a necessary condition of peace.

Thus, in his lonely and troubled childhood, William had been schooled for the rule of men. He had now, in the rule of a smaller dominion, in warfare and conquest on a smaller scale, to be schooled for the conquest and the rule of a greater dominion. William had the gifts of a born ruler and he was in no way disposed to abuse them. We know his rule in Normandy only through the language of panegyric; but the facts speak for themselves. He made Normandy peaceful and flourishing, more peaceful and flourishing perhaps than any other state of the European mainland. He is set before us as in everything a wise and beneficent ruler, the protector of the poor and helpless, the patron of commerce and of all that might profit his dominions. For defensive wars, for wars waged as the faithful man of his overlord, we cannot blame him. But his main duty lay at home. He still had revolts to put down, and he put them down. But to put them down was the first of good works. He had to keep the peace of the land, to put some check on the unruly wills of those turbulent barons on whom only an arm like his could put any check. He had, in the language of his day, to do justice, to visit wrong with sure and speedy punishment, whoever was the wrong-doer. If a ruler did this first of duties well, much was easily forgiven him in other ways. But William had as yet little to be forgiven. Throughout life he steadily practised some unusual virtues. His strict attention to religion was always marked. And his religion was not that mere lavish bounty to the Church which was consistent with any amount of cruelty or license. William's religion really influenced his life, public and private. He set an unusual example of a princely household governed according to the rules of morality, and he dealt with ecclesiastical matters in the spirit of a true reformer. He did not, like so many princes of his age, make ecclesiastical preferments a source of corrupt gain, but promoted good men from all quarters. His own education is not likely to have received much attention; it is not clear whether he had mastered the rarer art of writing or the more usual one of reading; but both his promotion of learned churchmen and the care given to the education of some of his children show that he at least valued the best attainments of his time. Had William's whole life been spent in the duties of a Norman duke, ruling his duchy wisely, defending it manfully, the world might never have known him for one of its foremost men, but his life on that narrower field would have been useful and honourable almost without a drawback. It was the fatal temptation of princes, the temptation to territorial aggrandizement, which enabled him fully to show the powers that were in him, but which at the same time led to his moral degradation. The defender of his own land became the invader of other lands, and the invader could not fail often to sink into the oppressor. Each step in his career as Conqueror was a step downwards. Maine was a neighbouring land, a land of the same speech, a land which, if the feelings of the time could have allowed a willing union, would certainly have lost nothing by an union with Normandy. England, a land apart, a land of speech, laws, and feelings, utterly unlike those of any part of Gaul, was in another case. There the Conqueror was driven to be the oppressor. Wrong, as ever, was punished by leading to further wrong.

With the two fields, nearer and more distant, narrower and wider, on which William was to appear as Conqueror he has as yet nothing to do. It is vain to guess at what moment the thought of the English succession may have entered his mind or that of his advisers. When William began his real reign after Val-ès-dunes, Norman influence was high in England. Edward the Confessor had spent his youth among his Norman kinsfolk; he loved Norman ways and the company of Normans and other men of French speech. Strangers from the favoured lands held endless posts in Church and State; above all, Robert of Jumièges, first Bishop of London and then Archbishop of Canterbury, was the King's special favourite and adviser. These men may have suggested the thought of William's succession very early. On the other hand, at this time it was by no means clear that Edward might not leave a son of his own. He had been only a few years married, and his alleged vow of chastity is very doubtful. William's claim was of the flimsiest kind. By English custom the king was chosen out of a single kingly house, and only those who were descended from kings in the male line were counted as members of that house. William was not descended, even in the female line, from any English king; his whole kindred with Edward was that Edward's mother Emma, a daughter of Richard the Fearless, was William's great-aunt. Such a kindred, to say nothing of William's bastardy, could give no right to the crown according to any doctrine of succession that ever was heard of. It could at most point him out as a candidate for adoption, in case the reigning king should be disposed and allowed to choose his successor. William or his advisers may have begun to weigh this chance very early; but all that is really certain is that William was a friend and favourite of his elder kinsman, and that events finally brought his succession to the English crown within the range of things that might be.

But, before this, William was to show himself as a warrior beyond the bounds of his own duchy, and to take seizin, as it were, of his great continental conquest. William's first war out of Normandy was waged in common with King Henry against Geoffrey Martel Count of Anjou, and waged on the side of Maine. William undoubtedly owed a debt of gratitude to his overlord for good help given at Val-ès-dunes, and excuses were never lacking for a quarrel between Anjou and Normandy. Both powers asserted rights over the intermediate land of Maine. In 1048 we find William giving help to Henry in a war with Anjou, and we hear wonderful but vague tales of his exploits. The really instructive part of the story deals with two border fortresses on the march of Normandy and Maine. Alençon lay on the Norman side of the Sarthe; but it was disloyal to Normandy. Brionne was still holding out for Guy of Burgundy. The town was a lordship of the house of Bellême, a house renowned for power and wickedness, and which, as holding great possessions alike of Normandy and of France, ranked rather with princes than with ordinary nobles. The story went that William Talvas, lord of Bellême, one of the fiercest of his race, had cursed William in his cradle, as one by whom he and his should be brought to shame. Such a tale set forth the noblest side of William's character, as the man who did something to put down such enemies of mankind as he who cursed him. The possessions of William Talvas passed through his daughter Mabel to Roger of Montgomery, a man who plays a great part in William's history; but it is the disloyalty of the burghers, not of their lord, of which we hear just now. They willingly admitted an Angevin garrison. William in return laid siege to Domfront on the Varenne, a strong castle which was then an outpost of Maine against Normandy. A long skirmishing warfare, in which William won for himself a name by deeds of personal prowess, went on during the autumn and winter (1048-49). One tale specially illustrates more than one point in the feelings of the time. The two princes, William and Geoffrey, give a mutual challenge; each gives the other notice of the garb and shield that he will wear that he may not be mistaken. The spirit of knight-errantry was coming in, and we see that William himself in his younger days was touched by it. But we see also that coat-armour was as yet unknown. Geoffrey and his host, so the Normans say, shrink from the challenge and decamp in the night, leaving the way open for a sudden march upon Alençon. The disloyal burghers received the duke with mockery of his birth. They hung out skins, and shouted, "Hides for the Tanner." Personal insult is always hard for princes to bear, and the wrath of William was stirred up to a pitch which made him for once depart from his usual moderation towards conquered enemies. He swore that the men who had jeered at him should be dealt with like a tree whose branches are cut off with the pollarding-knife. The town was taken by assault, and William kept his oath. The castle held out; the hands and feet of thirty-two pollarded burghers of Alençon were thrown over its walls, and the threat implied drove the garrison to surrender on promise of safety for life and limb. The defenders of Domfront, struck with fear, surrendered also, and kept their arms as well as their lives and limbs. William had thus won back his own rebellious town, and had enlarged his borders by his first conquest. He went farther south, and fortified another castle at Ambrières; but Ambrières was only a temporary conquest. Domfront has ever since been counted as part of Normandy. But, as ecclesiastical divisions commonly preserve the secular divisions of an earlier time, Domfront remained down to the great French Revolution in the spiritual jurisdiction of the bishops of Le Mans.

William had now shown himself in Maine as conqueror, and he was before long to show himself in England, though not yet as conqueror. If our chronology is to be trusted, he had still in this interval to complete his conquest of his own duchy by securing the surrender of Brionne; and two other events, both characteristic, one of them memorable, fill up the same time. William now banished a kinsman of his own name, who held the great county of Mortain, *Moretoliam* or *Moretonium*, in the diocese of Avranches, which must be carefully distinguished from Mortagne-en-Perche, *Mauritania* or *Moretonia* in the diocese of Seez. This act, of somewhat doubtful justice, is noteworthy on two grounds. First, the accuser of the banished count was one who was then a poor serving-knight of his own, but who became the forefather of a house which plays a great part in English history, Robert surnamed the Bigod. Secondly, the vacant county was granted by William to his own half-brother Robert. He had already in 1048 bestowed the bishopric of Bayeux on his other half-brother Odo, who cannot at that time have been more than twelve years old. He must therefore have held the see for a good while without consecration, and at no time of his fifty years' holding of it did he show any very episcopal merits. This was the last case in William's reign of an old abuse by which the chief church preferments in Normandy had been turned into means of providing for members, often unworthy members, of the ducal family; and it is the only one for which William can have been personally responsible. Both his brothers were thus placed very early in life among the chief men of Normandy, as they were in later years to be placed among the chief men of England. But William's affection for his brothers, amiable as it may have been personally, was assuredly not among the brighter parts of his character as a sovereign.

The other chief event of this time also concerns the domestic side of William's life. The long story of his marriage now begins. The date is fixed by one of the decrees of the council of Rheims held in 1049 by Pope Leo the Ninth, in which Baldwin Count of Flanders is forbidden to give his daughter to William the Norman. This implies that the marriage was already thought of, and further that it was looked on as uncanonical. The bride whom William sought, Matilda daughter of Baldwin the Fifth, was connected with him by some tie of kindred or affinity which made a marriage between them unlawful by the rules of the Church. But no genealogist has yet been able to find out exactly what the canonical hindrance was. It is hard to trace the descent of William and Matilda up to any common forefather. But the light which the story throws on William's character is the same in any case. Whether he was seeking a wife or a kingdom, he would have his will, but he could wait for it. In William's doubtful position, a marriage with the daughter of the Count of Flanders would be useful to him in many ways; and Matilda won her husband's abiding love and trust. Strange tales are told of William's wooing. Tales are told also of Matilda's earlier love for the Englishman Brihtric, who is said to have found favour in her eyes when he came as envoy from England to her father's court. All that is certain is that the marriage had been thought of and had been forbidden before the next important event in William's life that we have to record.

Was William's Flemish marriage in any way connected with his hopes of succession to the English crown? Had there been any available bride for him in England, it might have been for his interest to seek for her there. But it should be noticed, though no ancient writer points out the fact, that Matilda was actually descended from Alfred in the female line; so that William's children, though not William himself, had some few drops of English blood in their veins. William or his advisers, in weighing every chance which might help his interests in the direction of England, may have reckoned this piece of rather ancient genealogy among the advantages of a Flemish alliance. But it is far more certain that, between the forbidding of the marriage and the marriage itself, a direct hope of succession to the English crown had been opened to the Norman duke.

CHAPTER III—WILLIAM'S FIRST VISIT TO ENGLAND—A.D. 1051-1052

While William was strengthening himself in Normandy, Norman influence in England had risen to its full height. The king was surrounded by foreign favourites. The only foreign earl was his nephew Ralph of Mentes, the son of his sister Godgifu. But three chief bishoprics were held by Normans, Robert of Canterbury, William of London, and Ulf of Dorchester. William bears a good character, and won the esteem of Englishmen; but the unlearned Ulf is emphatically said to have done "nought bishoplike." Smaller preferments in Church and State, estates in all parts of the kingdom, were lavishly granted to strangers. They built castles, and otherwise gave offence to English feeling. Archbishop Robert, above all, was ever plotting against Godwine, Earl of the West-Saxons, the head of the national party. At last, in the autumn of 1051, the national indignation burst forth. The immediate occasion was a visit paid to the King by Count Eustace of Boulogne, who had just married the widowed Countess Godgifu. The violent dealings of his followers towards the burghers of

Dover led to resistance on their part, and to a long series of marches and negotiations, which ended in the banishment of Godwine and his son, and the parting of his daughter Edith, the King's wife, from her husband. From October 1051 to September 1052, the Normans had their own way in England. And during that time King Edward received a visitor of greater fame than his brother-in-law from Boulogne in the person of his cousin from Rouen.

Of his visit we only read that "William Earl came from beyond sea with mickle company of Frenchmen, and the king him received, and as many of his comrades as to him seemed good, and let him go again." Another account adds that William received great gifts from the King. But William himself in several documents speaks of Edward as his lord; he must therefore at some time have done to Edward an act of homage, and there is no time but this at which we can conceive such an act being done. Now for what was the homage paid? Homage was often paid on very trifling occasions, and strange conflicts of allegiance often followed. No such conflict was likely to arise if the Duke of the Normans, already the man of the King of the French for his duchy, became the man of the King of the English on any other ground. Betwixt England and France there was as yet no enmity or rivalry. England and France became enemies afterwards because the King of the English and the Duke of the Normans were one person. And this visit, this homage, was the first step towards making the King of the English and the Duke of the Normans the same person. The claim William had to the English crown rested mainly on an alleged promise of the succession made by Edward. This claim is not likely to have been a mere shameless falsehood. That Edward did make some promise to William —as that Harold, at a later stage, did take some oath to William—seems fully proved by the fact that, while such Norman statements as could be denied were emphatically denied by the English writers, on these two points the most patriotic Englishmen, the strongest partisans of Harold, keep a marked silence. We may be sure therefore that some promise was made; for that promise a time must be found, and no time seems possible except this time of William's visit to Edward. The date rests on no direct authority, but it answers every requirement. Those who spoke of the promise as being made earlier, when William and Edward were boys together in Normandy, forgot that Edward was many years older than William. The only possible moment earlier than the visit was when Edward was elected king in 1042. Before that time he could hardly have thought of disposing of a kingdom which was not his, and at that time he might have looked forward to leaving sons to succeed him. Still less could the promise have been made later than the visit. From 1053 to the end of his life Edward was under English influences, which led him first to send for his nephew Edward from Hungary as his successor, and in the end to make a recommendation in favour of Harold. But in 1051-52 Edward, whether under a vow or not, may well have given up the hope of children; he was surrounded by Norman influences; and, for the only time in the last twenty-four years of their joint lives, he and William met face to face. The only difficulty is one to which no contemporary writer makes any reference. If Edward wished to dispose of his crown in favour of one of his French-speaking kinsmen, he had a nearer kinsman of whom he might more naturally have thought. His own nephew Ralph was living in England and holding an English earldom. He had the advantage over both William and his own older brother Walter of Mantes, in not being a reigning prince elsewhere. We can only say that there is evidence that Edward did think of William, that there is no evidence that he ever thought of Ralph. And, except the tie of nearer kindred, everything would suggest William rather than Ralph. The personal comparison is almost grotesque; and Edward's early associations and the strongest influences around him, were not vaguely French but specially Norman. Archbishop Robert would plead for his own native sovereign only. In short, we may be as nearly sure as we can be of any fact for which there is no direct authority, that Edward's promise to William was made at the time of William's visit to England, and that William's homage to Edward was done in the character of a destined successor to the English crown.

William then came to England a mere duke and went back to Normandy a king expectant. But the value of his hopes, to the value of the promise made to him, are quite another matter. Most likely they were rated on both sides far above their real value. King and duke may both have believed that they were making a settlement which the English nation was bound to respect. If so, Edward at least was undeceived within a few months.

The notion of a king disposing of his crown by his own act belongs to the same range of ideas as the law of strict hereditary succession. It implies that kingship is a possession and not an office. Neither the heathen nor the Christian English had ever admitted that doctrine; but it was fast growing on the continent. Our forefathers had always combined respect for the kingly house with some measure of choice among the members of that house. Edward himself was not the lawful heir according to the notions of a modern lawyer; for he was chosen while the son of his elder brother was living. Every English king held his crown by the gift of the great assembly of the nation, though the choice of the nation was usually limited to the descendants of former kings, and though the full-grown son of the late king was seldom opposed. Christianity had strengthened the election principle. The king lost his old sanctity as the son of Woden; he gained a new sanctity as the Lord's anointed. But kingship thereby became more distinctly an office, a great post, like a bishopric, to which its holder had to be lawfully chosen and admitted by solemn rites. But of that office he could be lawfully deprived, nor could he hand it on to a successor either according to his own will or according to any strict law of succession. The wishes of the late king, like the wishes of the late bishop, went for something with the electors. But that was all. All that Edward could really do for his kinsmen was to promise to make, when the time came, a recommendation to the Witan in his favour. The Witan might then deal as they thought good with a recommendation so unusual as to choose to the kingship of England a man who was neither a native nor a conqueror of England nor the descendant of any English king.

When the time came, Edward did make a recommendation to the

Witan, but it was not in favour of William. The English influences under which he was brought during his last fourteen years taught him better what the law of England was and what was the duty of an English king. But at the time of William's visit Edward may well have believed that he could by his own act settle his crown on his Norman kinsman as his undoubted successor in case he died without a son. And it may be that Edward was bound by a vow not to leave a son. And if Edward so thought, William naturally thought so yet more; he would sincerely believe himself to be the lawful heir of the crown of England, the sole lawful successor, except in one contingency which was perhaps impossible and certainly unlikely.

The memorials of these times, so full on some points, are meagre on others. Of those writers who mention the bequest or promise none mention it at any time when it is supposed to have happened; they mention it at some later time when it began to be of practical importance. No English writer speaks of William's claim till the time when he was about practically to assert it; no Norman writer speaks of it till he tells the tale of Harold's visit and oath to William. We therefore cannot say how far the promise was known either in England or on the continent. But it could not be kept altogether hid, even if either party wished it to be hid. English statesmen must have known of it, and must have guided their policy accordingly, whether it was generally known in the country or not. William's position, both in his own duchy and among neighbouring princes, would be greatly improved if he could be looked upon as a future king. As heir to the crown of England, he may have more earnestly wooed the descendant of former wearers of the crown; and Matilda and her father may have looked more favourably on a suitor to whom the crown of England was promised. On the other hand, the existence of such a foreign claimant made it more needful than ever for Englishmen to be ready with an English successor, in the royal house or out of it, the moment the reigning king should pass away.

It was only for a short time that William could have had any reasonable hope of a peaceful succession. The time of Norman influence in England was short. The revolution of September 1052 brought Godwine back, and placed the rule of England again in English hands. Many Normans were banished, above all Archbishop Robert and Bishop Ulf. The death of Godwine the next year placed the chief power in the hands of his son Harold. This change undoubtedly made Edward more disposed to the national cause. Of Godwine, the man to whom he owed his crown, he was clearly in awe; to Godwine's sons he was personally attached. We know not how Edward was led to look on his promise to William as void. That he was so led is quite plain. He sent for his nephew the Ætheling Edward from Hungary, clearly as his intended successor. When the Ætheling died in 1057, leaving a son under age, men seem to have gradually come to look to Harold as the probable successor. He clearly held a special position above that of an ordinary earl; but there is no need to suppose any formal act in his favour till the time of the King's death, January 5, 1066. On his deathbed Edward did all that he legally could do on behalf of Harold by recommending him to the Witan for election as the next king. That he then either made a new or renewed an old nomination in favour of William is a fable which is set aside by the witness of the contemporary English writers. William's claim rested wholly on that earlier nomination which could hardly have been made at any other time than his visit to England.

We have now to follow William back to Normandy, for the remaining years of his purely ducal reign. The expectant king had doubtless thoughts and hopes which he had not had before. But we can guess at them only: they are not recorded.

CHAPTER IV—THE REIGN OF WILLIAM IN NORMANDY—A.D. 1052-1063

If William came back from England looking forward to a future crown, the thought might even then flash across his mind that he was not likely to win that crown without fighting for it. As yet his business was still to fight for the duchy of Normandy. But he had now to fight, not to win his duchy, but only to keep it. For five years he had to strive both against rebellious subjects and against invading enemies, among whom King Henry of Paris is again the foremost. Whatever motives had led the French king to help William at Val-ès-dunes had now passed away. He had fallen back on his former state of abiding enmity towards Normandy and her duke. But this short period definitely fixed the position of Normandy and her duke in Gaul and in Europe. At its beginning William is still the Bastard of Falaise, who may or may not be able to keep himself in the ducal chair, his right to which is still disputed. At the end of it, if he is not yet the Conqueror and the Great, he has shown all the gifts that were needed to win him either name. He is the greatest vassal of the French crown, a vassal more powerful than the overlord whose invasions of his duchy he has had to drive back.

These invasions of Normandy by the King of the French and his allies fall into two periods. At first Henry appears in Normandy as the supporter of Normans in open revolt against their duke. But revolts are personal and local; there is no rebellion like that which was crushed at Val-ès-dunes, spreading over a large part of the duchy. In the second period, the invaders have no such starting-point. There are still traitors; there are still rebels; but all that they can do is to join the invaders after they have entered the land. William is still only making his way to the universal good will of his duchy: but he is fast making it.

There is, first of all, an obscure tale of a revolt of an unfixed date, but which must have happened between 1048 and 1053. The rebel, William Busac of the house of Eu, is said to have defended the castle of Eu against the duke and to have gone into banishment in France. But the year that followed William's visit to England saw the far more memorable revolt of William Count of Arques. He had drawn the Duke's suspicions on him, and he had to receive a ducal garrison in his great fortress by Dieppe. But the garrison betrayed the castle to its own master. Open revolt and havoc followed, in which Count William was supported by the king and by several other princes. Among them was Ingelram Count of Ponthieu, husband of the duke's sister Adelaide. Another enemy was Guy Count of Gascony, afterwards Duke William the Eighth of Aquitaine. What quarrel a prince in the furthest corner of Gaul could have with the Duke of the Normans does not appear; but neither Count William nor his allies could withstand the loyal Normans and their prince. Count Ingelram was killed; the other princes withdrew to devise greater efforts against Normandy. Count William lost his castle and part of his estates, and left the duchy of his free will. The Duke's politic forbearance at last won him the general good will of his subjects. We hear of no more open revolts till that of William's own son many years after. But the assaults of foreign enemies, helped sometimes by Norman traitors, begin again the next year on a greater scale.

William the ruler and warrior had now a short breathing-space. He had doubtless come back from England more bent than ever on his marriage with Matilda of Flanders. Notwithstanding the decree of a Pope and a Council entitled to special respect, the marriage was celebrated, not very long after William's return to Normandy, in the year of the revolt of William of Arques. In the course of the year 1053 Count Baldwin brought his daughter to the Norman frontier at Eu, and there she became the bride of William. We know not what emboldened William to risk so daring a step at this particular time, or what led Baldwin to consent to it. If it was suggested by the imprisonment of Pope Leo by William's countrymen in Italy, in the hope that a consent to the marriage would be wrung out of the captive pontiff, that hope was disappointed. The marriage raised much opposition in Normandy. It was denounced by Archbishop Malger of Rouen, the brother of the dispossessed Count of Arques. His character certainly added no weight to his censures; but the same act in a saint would have been set down as a sign of holy boldness. Presently, whether for his faults or for his merits, Malger was deposed in a synod of the Norman Church, and William found him a worthier successor in the learned and holy Maurilius. But a greater man than Malger also opposed the marriage, and the controversy thus introduces us to one who fills a place second only to that of William himself in the Norman and English history of the time.

This was Lanfranc of Pavia, the lawyer, the scholar, the model monk, the ecclesiastical statesman, who, as prior of the newly founded abbey of Bec, was already one of the innermost counsellors of the Duke. As duke and king, as prior, abbot, and archbishop, William and Lanfranc ruled side by side, each helping the work of the other till the end of their joint lives. Once only, at this time, was their friendship broken for a moment. Lanfranc spoke against the marriage, and ventured to rebuke the Duke himself. William's wrath was kindled; he ordered Lanfranc into banishment and took a baser revenge by laying waste part of the lands of the abbey. But the quarrel was soon made up. Lanfranc presently left Normandy, not as a banished man, but as the envoy of its sovereign, commissioned to work for the confirmation of the marriage at the papal court. He worked, and his work was crowned with success, but not with speedy success. It was not till six years after the marriage, not till the year 1059, that Lanfranc obtained the wished for confirmation, not from Leo, but from his remote successor Nicolas the Second. The sin of those who had contracted the unlawful union was purged by various good works, among which the foundation of the two stately abbeys of Caen was conspicuous.

This story illustrates many points in the character of William and of his time. His will is not to be thwarted, whether in a matter of marriage or of any other. But he does not hurry matters; he waits for a favourable opportunity. Something, we know not what, must have made the year 1053 more favourable than the year 1049. We mark also William's relations to the Church. He is at no time disposed to submit quietly to the bidding of the spiritual power, when it interferes with his rights or even when it crosses his will. Yet he is really anxious for ecclesiastical reform; he promotes men like Maurilius and Lanfranc; perhaps he is not displeased when the exercise of ecclesiastical discipline, in the case of Malger, frees him from a troublesome censor. But the worse side of him also comes out. William could forgive rebels, but he could not bear the personal rebuke even of his friend. Under this feeling he punishes a whole body of men for the offence of one. To lay waste the lands of Bec for the rebuke of Lanfranc was like an ordinary prince of the time; it was unlike William, if he had not been stirred up by a censure which touched his wife as well as himself. But above all, the bargain between William and Lanfranc is characteristic of the man and the age. Lanfranc goes to Rome to support a marriage which he had censured in Normandy. But there is no formal inconsistency, no forsaking of any principle. Lanfranc holds an uncanonical marriage to be a sin, and he denounces it. He does not withdraw his judgement as to its sinfulness. He simply uses his influence with a power that can forgive the sin to get it forgiven.

While William's marriage was debated at Rome, he had to fight hard in Normandy. His warfare and his negotiations ended about the same time, and the two things may have had their bearing on one another. William had now to undergo a new form of trial. The King of the French had never put forth his full strength when he was simply backing Norman rebels. William had now, in two successive invasions, to withstand the whole power of the King, and of as many of his vassals as the King could bring to his standard. In the first invasion, in 1054, the Norman writers speak rhetorically of warriors from Burgundy, Auvergne, and Gascony; but it is hard to see any troops from a greater distance than Bourges. The princes who followed Henry seem to have been only the nearer vassals of the Crown. Chief among them are Theobald Count of Chartres, of a house of old hostile to Normandy, and Guy the new Count of Ponthieu, to be often heard of again. If not Geoffrey of Anjou himself, his subjects from Tours were also there. Normandy was to be invaded on two sides, on both banks of the Seine. The King and his allies sought to wrest from William the western part of Normandy, the older and the more thoroughly French part. No attack seems to have been designed on the Bessin or the Côtentin. William was to be allowed to keep those parts of his duchy, against which he had to fight when the King was his ally at Val-ès-dunes.

The two armies entered Normandy; that which was to act on the left of the Seine was led by the King, the other by his brother Odo. Against the King William made ready to act himself; eastern Normandy was left to its own loyal nobles. But all Normandy was now loyal; the men of the Saxon and Danish lands were as ready to fight for their duke against the King as they had been to fight against King and Duke together. But William avoided pitched battles; indeed pitched battles are rare in the continental warfare of the time. War consists largely in surprises, and still more in the attack and defence of fortified places. The plan of William's present campaign was wholly defensive; provisions and cattle were to be carried out of the French line of march; the Duke on his side, the other Norman leaders on the other side, were to watch the enemy and attack them at any favourable moment. The commanders east of the Seine, Count Robert of Eu, Hugh of Gournay, William Crispin, and Walter Giffard, found their opportunity when the French had entered the unfortified town of Mortemer and had given themselves up to revelry. Fire and sword did the work. The whole French army was slain, scattered, or taken prisoners. Ode escaped; Guy of Ponthieu was taken. The Duke's success was still easier. The tale runs that the news from Mortemer, suddenly announced to the King's army in the dead of the night, struck them with panic, and led to a hasty retreat out of the land.

This campaign is truly Norman; it is wholly unlike the simple warfare of England. A traitorous Englishman did nothing or helped the enemy; a patriotic Englishman gave battle to the enemy the first time he had a chance. But no English commander of the eleventh century was likely to lay so subtle a plan as this, and, if he had laid such a plan, he would hardly have found an English army able to carry it out. Harold, who refused to lay waste a rood of English ground, would hardly have looked quietly on while many roods of English ground were wasted by the enemy. With all the valour of the Normans, what before all things distinguished them from other nations was their craft. William could indeed fight a pitched battle when a pitched battle served his purpose; but he could control himself, he could control his followers, even to the point of enduring to look quietly on the havoc of their own land till the right moment. He who could do this was indeed practising for his calling as Conqueror. And if the details of the story, details specially characteristic, are to be believed, William showed something also of that grim pleasantry which was another marked feature in the Norman character. The startling message which struck the French army with panic was deliberately sent with that end. The messenger sent climbs a tree or a rock, and, with a voice as from another world, bids the French awake; they are sleeping too long; let them go and bury their friends who are lying dead at Mortemer. These touches bring home to us the character of the man and the people with whom our forefathers had presently to deal. William was the greatest of his race, but he was essentially of his race; he was Norman to the backbone.

Of the French army one division had been surprised and cut to pieces, the other had left Normandy without striking a blow. The war was not yet quite over; the French still kept Tillières; William accordingly fortified the stronghold of Breteuil as a cheek upon it. And he entrusted the command to a man who will soon be memorable, his personal friend William, son of his old guardian Osbern. King Henry was now glad to conclude a peace on somewhat remarkable terms. William had the king's leave to take what he could from Count Geoffrey of Anjou. He now annexed Cenomannian— that is just now Angevin—territory at more points than one, but chiefly on the line of his earlier advances to Domfront and Ambrières. Ambrières had perhaps been lost; for William now sent Geoffrey a challenge to come on the fortieth day. He came on the fortieth day, and found Ambrières strongly fortified and occupied by a Norman garrison. With Geoffrey came the Breton prince Ode, and William or Peter Duke of Aquitaine. They besieged the castle; but Norman accounts add that they all fled on William's approach to relieve it.

Three years of peace now followed, but in 1058 King Henry, this time in partnership with Geoffrey of Anjou, ventured another invasion of Normandy. He might say that he had never been fairly beaten in his former campaign, but that he had been simply cheated out of the land by Norman wiles. This time he had a second experience of Norman wiles and of Norman strength too. King and Count entered the land and ravaged far and wide. William, as before, allowed the enemy to waste the land. He watched and followed them till he found a favourable moment for attack. The people in general zealously helped the Duke's schemes, but some traitors of rank were still leagued with the Count of Anjou. While William bided his time, the invaders burned Caen. This place, so famous in Norman history, was not one of the ancient cities of the land. It was now merely growing into importance, and it was as yet undefended by walls or castle. But when the ravagers turned eastward, William found the opportunity that he had waited for. As the French were crossing the ford of Varaville on the Dive, near the mouth of that river, he came suddenly on them, and slaughtered a large part of the army under the eyes of the king who had already crossed. The remnant marched out of Normandy.

Henry now made peace, and restored Tillières. Not long after, in 1060, the King died, leaving his young son Philip, who had been already crowned, as his successor, under the guardianship of William's father-in-law Baldwin. Geoffrey of Anjou and William of Aquitaine also died, and the Angevin power was weakened by the division of Geoffrey's dominions between his nephews. William's position was greatly strengthened, now that France, under the new regent, had become friendly, while Anjou was no longer able to do mischief. William had now nothing to fear from his neighbours, and the way was soon opened for his great continental conquest. But what effect had these events on William's views on England? About the time of the second French invasion of Normandy Earl Harold became beyond doubt the first man in England, and for the first time a chance of the royal succession was opened to him. In 1057, the year before Varaville, the Ætheling Edward, the King's selected successor, died soon after his coming to England; in the same year died the King's nephew Earl Ralph and Leofric Earl of the Mercians, the only Englishmen whose influence could at all compare with that of Harold. Harold's succession now became possible; it became even likely, if Edward should die while Edgar the son of the Ætheling was still under age. William had no shadow of excuse for interfering, but he doubtless was watching the internal affairs of England. Harold was certainly watching the affairs of Gaul. About this time, most likely in the year 1058, he made a pilgrimage to Rome, and on his way back he looked diligently into the state of things among the various vassals of the French crown. His exact purpose is veiled in ambiguous language; but we can hardly doubt that his object was to contract alliances with the continental enemies of Normandy. Such views looked to the distant future, as William had as yet been guilty of no unfriendly act towards England. But it was well to come to an understanding with King Henry, Count Geoffrey, and Duke William of Aquitaine, in case a time should come when their interests and those of England would be the same. But the deaths of all those princes must have put an end to all hopes of common action between England and any Gaulish power. The Emperor Henry also, the firm ally of England, was dead. It was now clear that, if England should ever have to withstand a Norman attack, she would have to withstand it wholly by her own strength, or with such help as she might find among the kindred powers of the North.

William's great continental conquest is drawing nigh; but between the campaign of Varaville and the campaign of Le Mans came the tardy papal confirmation of William's marriage. The Duke and Duchess, now at last man and wife in the eye of the Church, began to carry out the works of penance which were allotted to them. The abbeys of Caen, William's Saint Stephen's, Matilda's Holy Trinity, now began to arise. Yet, at this moment of reparation, one or two facts seem to place William's government of his duchy in a less favourable light than usual. The last French invasion was followed by confiscations and banishments among the chief men of Normandy. Roger of Montgomery and his wife Mabel, who certainly was capable of any deed of blood or treachery, are charged with acting as false accusers. We see also that, as late as the day of Varaville, there were Norman traitors. Robert of Escalfoy had taken the Angevin side, and had defended his castle against the Duke. He died in a strange way, after snatching an apple from the hand of his own wife. His nephew Arnold remained in rebellion three years, and was simply required to go to the wars in Apulia. It is hard to believe that the Duke had poisoned the apple, if poisoned it was; but finding treason still at work among his nobles, he may have too hastily listened to charges against men who had done him good service, and who were to do him good service again.

Five years after the combat at Varaville, William really began to deserve, though not as yet to receive, the name of Conqueror. For he now did a work second only to the conquest of England. He won the city of Le Mans and the whole land of Maine. Between the tale of Maine and the tale of England there is much of direct likeness. Both lands were won against the will of their inhabitants; but both conquests were made with an elaborate show of legal right. William's earlier conquests in Maine had been won, not from any count of Maine, but from Geoffrey of Anjou, who had occupied the country to the prejudice of two successive counts, Hugh and Herbert. He had further imprisoned the Bishop of Le Mans, Gervase of the house of Bellême, though the King of the French had at his request granted to the Count of Anjou for life royal rights over the bishopric of Le Mans. The bishops of Le Mans, who thus, unlike the bishops of Normandy, held their temporalities of the distant king and not of the local count, held a very independent position. The citizens of Le Mans too had large privileges and a high spirit to defend them; the city was in a marked way the head of the district. Thus it commonly carried with it the action of the whole country. In Maine there were three rival powers, the prince, the Church, and the people. The position of the counts was further weakened by the claims to their homage made by the princes on either side of them in Normandy and Anjou; the position of the Bishop, vassal, till Gervase's late act, of the King only, was really a higher one. Geoffrey had been received at Le Mans with the good will of the citizens, and both Bishop and Count sought shelter with William. Gervase was removed from the strife by promotion to the highest place in the French kingdom, the archbishopric of Rheims. The young Count Herbert, driven from his county, commended himself to William. He became his man; he agreed to hold his dominions of him, and to marry one of his daughters. If he died childless, his father-in-law was to take the fief into his own hands. But to unite the old and new dynasties, Herbert's youngest sister Margaret was to marry William's eldest son Robert. If female descent went for anything, it is not clear why Herbert passed by the rights of his two elder sisters, Gersendis, wife of Azo Marquess of Liguria, and Paula, wife of John of La Flèche on the borders of Maine and Anjou. And sons both of Gersendis and of Paula did actually reign at Le Mans, while no child either of Herbert or of Margaret ever came into being.

If Herbert ever actually got possession of his country, his possession of it was short. He died in 1063 before either of the contemplated marriages had been carried out. William therefore stood towards Maine as he expected to stand with regard to England. The sovereign of each country had made a formal settlement of his dominions in his favour. It was to be seen whether those who were most immediately concerned would accept that settlement. Was the rule either of Maine or of England to be handed over in this way, like a mere property, without the people who were to be ruled speaking their minds on the matter? What the people of England said to this question in 1066 we shall hear presently; what the people of Maine said in 1063 we hear now. We know not why they had submitted to the Angevin count; they had now no mind to merge their country in the dominions of the Norman duke. The Bishop was neutral; but the nobles and the citizens of Le Mans were of one mind in refusing William's demand to be received as count by virtue of the agreement with Herbert. They chose rulers for themselves. Passing by Gersendis and Paula and their sons, they sent for Herbert's aunt Biota and her husband Walter Count of Mantes. Strangely enough, Walter, son of Godgifu daughter of Æthelred, was a possible, though not a likely, candidate for the rule of England as well as of Maine. The people of Maine are not likely to have thought of this bit of genealogy. But it was doubtless present to the minds alike of William and of Harold.

William thus, for the first but not for the last time, claimed the rule of a people who had no mind to have him as their ruler. Yet, morally worthless as were his claims over Maine, in the merely technical way of looking at things, he had more to say than most princes have who annex the lands of their neighbours. He had a perfectly good right by the terms of the agreement with Herbert. And it might be argued by any who admitted the Norman claim to the homage of Maine, that on the failure of male heirs the country reverted to the overlord. Yet female succession was now coming in. Anjou had passed to the sons of Geoffrey's sister; it had not fallen back to the French king. There was thus a twofold answer to William's claim, that Herbert could not grant away even the rights of his sisters, still less the rights of his people. Still it was characteristic of William that he had a case that might be plausibly argued. The people of Maine had fallen back on the old Teutonic right. They had chosen a prince connected with the old stock, but who was not the next heir according to any rule of succession. Walter was hardly worthy of such an exceptional honour; he showed no more energy in Maine than his brother Ralph had shown in England. The city was defended by Geoffrey, lord of Mayenne, a valiant man who fills a large place in the local history. But no valour or skill could withstand William's plan of warfare. He invaded Maine in much the same sort in which he had defended Normandy. He gave out that he wished to win Maine without shedding man's blood. He fought no battles; he did not attack the city, which he left to be the last spot that should be devoured. He harried the open country, he occupied the smaller posts, till the citizens were driven, against Geoffrey's will, to surrender. William entered Le Mans; he was received, we are told, with joy. When men make the best of a bad bargain, they sometimes persuade themselves that they are really pleased. William, as ever, shed no blood; he harmed none of the men who had become his subjects; but Le Mans was to be bridled; its citizens needed a castle and a Norman garrison to keep them in their new allegiance. Walter and Biota surrendered their claims on Maine and became William's guests at Falaise. Meanwhile Geoffrey of Mayenne refused to submit, and withstood the new Count of Maine in his stronghold. William laid siege to Mayenne, and took it by the favoured Norman argument of fire. All Maine was now in the hands of the Conqueror.

William had now made a greater conquest than any Norman duke had made before him. He had won a county and a noble city, and he had won them, in the ideas of his own age, with honour. Are we to believe that he sullied his conquest by putting his late competitors, his present guests, to death by poison? They died conveniently for him, and they died in his own house. Such a death was strange; but strange things do happen. William gradually came to shrink from no crime for which he could find a technical defence; but no advocate could have said anything on behalf of the poisoning of Walter and Biota. Another member of the house of Maine, Margaret the betrothed of his son Robert, died about the same time; and her at least William had every motive to keep alive. One who was more dangerous than Walter, if he suffered anything, only suffered banishment. Of Geoffrey of Mayenne we hear no more till William had again to fight for the possession of Maine.

William had thus, in the year 1063, reached the height of his power and fame as a continental prince. In a conquest on Gaulish soil he had rehearsed the greater conquest which he was before long to make beyond sea. Three years, eventful in England, outwardly uneventful in Normandy, still part us from William's second visit to our shores. But in the course of these three years one event must have happened, which, without a blow being struck or a treaty being signed, did more for his hopes than any battle or any treaty. At some unrecorded time, but at a time which must come within these years, Harold Earl of the West-Saxons became the guest and the man of William Duke of the Normans.

CHAPTER V—HAROLD'S OATH TO WILLIAM—A.D. 1064?

The lord of Normandy and Maine could now stop and reckon his chances of becoming lord of England also. While our authorities enable us to put together a fairly full account of both Norman and English events, they throw no light on the way in which men in either land looked at events in the other. Yet we might give much to know what William and Harold at this time thought of one another. Nothing had as yet happened to make the two great rivals either national or personal enemies. England and Normandy were at peace, and the great duke and the great earl had most likely had no personal dealings with one another. They were rivals in the sense that each looked forward to succeed to the English crown whenever the reigning king should die. But neither had as yet put forward his claim in any shape that the other could look on as any formal wrong to himself. If William and Harold had ever met, it could have been only during Harold's journey in Gaul. Whatever negotiations Harold made during that journey were negotiations unfriendly to William; still he may, in the course of that journey, have visited Normandy as well as France or Anjou. It is hard to avoid the thought that the tale of Harold's visit to William, of his oath to William, arose out of something that happened on Harold's way back from his Roman pilgrimage. To that journey we can give an approximate date. Of any other journey we have no date and no certain detail. We can say only that the fact that no English writer makes any mention of any such visit, of any such oath, is, under the circumstances, the strongest proof that the story of the visit and the oath has some kind of foundation. Yet if we grant thus much, the story reads on the whole as if it happened a few years later than the English earl's return from Rome.

It is therefore most likely that Harold did pay a second visit to Gaul, whether a first or a second visit to Normandy, at some time nearer to

Edward's death than the year 1058. The English writers are silent; the Norman writers give no date or impossible dates; they connect the visit with a war in Britanny; but that war is without a date. We are driven to choose the year which is least rich in events in the English annals. Harold could not have paid a visit of several months to Normandy either in 1063 or in 1065. Of those years the first was the year of Harold's great war in Wales, when he found how the Britons might be overcome by their own arms, when he broke the power of Gruffydd, and granted the Welsh kingdom to princes who became the men of Earl Harold as well as of King Edward. Harold's visit to Normandy is said to have taken place in the summer and autumn mouths; but the summer and autumn of 1065 were taken up by the building and destruction of Harold's hunting-seat in Wales and by the greater events of the revolt and pacification of Northumberland. But the year 1064 is a blank in the English annals till the last days of December, and no action of Harold's in that year is recorded. It is therefore the only possible year among those just before Edward's death. Harold's visit and oath to William may very well have taken place in that year; but that is all.

We know as little for certain as to the circumstances of the visit or the nature of the oath. We can say only that Harold did something which enabled William to charge him with perjury and breach of the duty of a vassal. It is inconceivable in itself, and unlike the formal scrupulousness of William's character, to fancy that he made his appeal to all Christendom without any ground at all. The Norman writers contradict one another so thoroughly in every detail of the story that we can look on no part of it as trustworthy. Yet such a story can hardly have grown up so near to the alleged time without some kernel of truth in it. And herein comes the strong corroborative witness that the English writers, denying every other charge against Harold, pass this one by without notice. We can hardly doubt that Harold swore some oath to William which he did not keep. More than this it would be rash to say except as an avowed guess.

As our nearest approach to fixing the date is to take that year which is not impossible, so, to fix the occasion of the visit, we can only take that one among the Norman versions which is also not impossible. All the main versions represent Harold as wrecked on the coast of Ponthieu, as imprisoned, according to the barbarous law of wreck, by Count Guy, and as delivered by the intervention of William. If any part of the story is true, this is. But as to the circumstances which led to the shipwreck there is no agreement. Harold assuredly was not sent to announce to William a devise of the crown in his favour made with the consent of the Witan of England and confirmed by the oaths of Stigand, Godwine, Siward, and Leofric. Stigand became Archbishop in September 1052: Godwine died at Easter 1053. The devise must therefore have taken place, and Harold's journey must have taken place, within those few most unlikely months, the very time when Norman influence was overthrown. Another version makes Harold go, against the King's warnings, to bring back his brother Wulfnoth and his nephew Hakon, who had been given as hostages on the return of Godwine, and had been entrusted by the King to the keeping of Duke William. This version is one degree less absurd; but no such hostages are known to have been given, and if they were, the patriotic party, in the full swing of triumph, would hardly have allowed them to be sent to Normandy. A third version makes Harold's presence the result of mere accident. He is sailing to Wales or Flanders, or simply taking his pleasure in the Channel, when he is cast by a storm on the coast of Ponthieu. Of these three accounts we may choose the third as the only one that is possible. It is also one out of which the others may have grown, while it is hard to see how the third could have arisen out of either of the others. Harold then, we may suppose, fell accidentally into the clutches of Guy, and was rescued from them, at some cost in ransom and in grants of land, by Guy's overlord Duke William.

The whole story is eminently characteristic of William. He would be honestly indignant at Guy's base treatment of Harold, and he would feel it his part as Guy's overlord to redress the wrong. But he would also be alive to the advantage of getting establish a claim to gratitude on the part of Harold would be something. But he might easily do more, and, according to all accounts, he did more. Harold, we are told, as the Duke's friend and guest, returns the obligation under which the Duke has laid him by joining him in one or more expeditions against the Bretons. The man who had just smitten the Bret-Welsh of the island might well be asked to fight, and might well be ready to fight, against the Bret-Welsh of the mainland. The services of Harold won him high honour; he was admitted into the ranks of Norman knighthood, and engaged to marry one of William's daughters. Now, at any time to which we can fix Harold's visit, all William's daughters must have been mere children. Harold, on the other hand, seems to have been a little older than William. Yet there is nothing unlikely in the engagement, and it is the one point in which all the different versions, contradicting each other on every other point, agree without exception. Whatever else Harold promises, he promises this, and in some versions he does not promise anything else.

Here then we surely have the kernel of truth round which a mass of fable, varying in different reports, has gathered. On no other point is there any agreement. The place is unfixed; half a dozen Norman towns and castles are made the scene of the oath. The form of the oath is unfixed; in some accounts it is the ordinary oath of homage; in others it is an oath of fearful solemnity, taken on the holiest relics. In one well-known account, Harold is even made to swear on hidden relics, not knowing on what he is swearing. Here is matter for much thought. To hold that one form of oath or promise is more binding than another upsets all true confidence between man and man. The notion of the specially binding nature of the oath by relies assumes that, in case of breach of the oath, every holy person to whose relies despite has been done will become the personal enemy of the perjurer. But the last story of all is the most instructive. William's formal, and more than formal, religion abhorred a false oath, in himself or in another man. But, so long as he keeps himself personally clear from the guilt, he does not scruple to put another man under special temptation, and, while believing in the power of the holy relics, he does not scruple to abuse them to a purpose of fraud. Surely, if Harold did break his oath, the wrath of the saints would fall more justly on William. Whether the tale be true or false, it equally illustrates the feelings of the time, and assuredly its truth or falsehood concerns the character of William far more than that of Harold.

What it was that Harold swore, whether in this specially solemn fashion or in any other, is left equally uncertain. In any case he engages to marry a daughter of William—as to which daughter the statements are endless—and in most versions he engages to do something more. He becomes the man of William, much as William had become the man of Edward. He promises to give his sister in marriage to an unnamed Norman baron. Moreover he promises to secure the kingdom of England for William at Edward's death. Perhaps he is himself to hold the kingdom or part of it under William; in any case William is to be the overlord; in the more usual story, William is to be himself the immediate king, with Harold as his highest and most favoured subject. Meanwhile Harold is to act in William's interest, to receive a Norman garrison in Dover castle, and to build other castles at other points. But no two stories agree, and not a few know nothing of anything beyond the promise of marriage.

Now if William really required Harold to swear to all these things, it must have been simply in order to have an occasion against him. If Harold really swore to all of them, it must have been simply because he felt that he was practically in William's power, without any serious intention of keeping the oath. If Harold took any such oath, he undoubtedly broke it; but we may safely say that any guilt on his part lay wholly in taking the oath, not in breaking it. For he swore to do what he could not do, and what it would have been a crime to do, if he could. If the King himself could not dispose of the crown, still less could the most powerful subject. Harold could at most promise William his "vote and interest," whenever the election came. But no one can believe that even Harold's influence could have obtained the crown for William. His influence lay in his being the embodiment of the national feeling; for him to appear as the supporter of William would have been to lose the crown for himself without gaining it for William. Others in England and in Scandinavia would have been glad of it. And the engagements to surrender Dover castle and the like were simply engagements on the part of an English earl to play the traitor against England. If William really called on Harold to swear to all this, he did so, not with any hope that the oath would be kept, but simply to put his competitor as far as possible in the wrong. But most likely Harold swore only to something much simpler. Next to the universal agreement about the marriage comes the very general agreement that Harold became William's man. In these two statements we have probably the whole truth. In those days men took the obligation of homage upon themselves very easily. Homage was no degradation, even in the highest; a man often did homage to any one from whom he had received any great benefit, and Harold had received a very great benefit from William. Nor did homage to a new lord imply treason to the old one. Harold, delivered by William from Guy's dungeon, would be eager to do for William any act of friendship. The homage would be little more than binding himself in the strongest form so to do. The relation of homage could be made to mean anything or nothing, as might be convenient. The man might often understand it in one sense and the lord in another. If Harold became the man of William, he would look on the act as little more than an expression of good will and gratitude towards his benefactor, his future father-in-law, his commander in the

Breton war. He would not look on it as forbidding him to accept the English crown if it were offered to him. Harold, the man of Duke William, might become a king, if he could, just as William, the man of King Philip, might become a king, if he could. As things went in those days, both the homage and the promise of marriage were capable of being looked on very lightly.

But it was not in the temper or in the circumstances of William to put any such easy meaning on either promise. The oath might, if needful, be construed very strictly, and William was disposed to construe it very strictly. Harold had not promised William a crown, which was not his to promise; but he had promised to do that which might be held to forbid him to take a crown which William held to be his own. If the man owed his lord any duty at all, it was surely his duty not to thwart his lord's wishes in such a matter. If therefore, when the vacancy of the throne came, Harold took the crown himself, or even failed to promote William's claim to it, William might argue that he had not rightly discharged the duty of a man to his lord. He could make an appeal to the world against the new king, as a perjured man, who had failed to help his lord in the matter where his lord most needed his help. And, if the oath really had been taken on relics of special holiness, he could further appeal to the religious feelings of the time against the man who had done despite to the saints. If he should be driven to claim the crown by arms, he could give the war the character of a crusade. All this in the end William did, and all this, we may be sure, he looked forward to doing, when he caused Harold to become his man. The mere obligation of homage would, in the skilful hands of William and Lanfranc, be quite enough to work on men's minds, as William wished to work on them. To Harold meanwhile and to those in England who heard the story, the engagement would not seem to carry any of these consequences. The mere homage then, which Harold could hardly refuse, would answer William's purpose nearly as well as any of these fuller obligations which Harold would surely have refused. And when a man older than William engaged to marry William's child-daughter, we must bear in mind the lightness with which such promises were made. William could not seriously expect that this engagement would be kept, if anything should lead Harold to another marriage. The promise was meant simply to add another count to the charges against Harold when the time should come. Yet on this point it is not clear that the oath was broken. Harold undoubtedly married Ealdgyth, daughter of Ælfgar and widow of Gruffydd and not any daughter of William. But in one version Harold is made to say that the daughter of William whom he had engaged to marry was dead. And that one of William's daughters did die very early there seems little doubt.

Whatever William did Lanfranc no doubt at least helped to plan. The Norman duke was subtle, but the Italian churchman was subtler still. In this long series of schemes and negotiations which led to the conquest of England, we are dealing with two of the greatest recorded masters of statecraft. We may call their policy dishonest and immoral, and so it was. But it was hardly more dishonest and immoral than most of the diplomacy of later times. William's object was, without any formal breach of faith on his own part, to entrap Harold into an engagement which might be understood in different senses, and which, in the sense which William chose to put upon it, Harold was sure to break. Two men, themselves of virtuous life, a rigid churchman and a layman of unusual religious strictness, do not scruple to throw temptation in the way of a fellow man in the hope that he will yield to that temptation. They exact a promise, because the promise is likely to be broken, and because its breach would suit their purposes. Through all William's policy a strong regard for formal right as he chose to understand formal right, is not only found in company with much practical wrong, but is made the direct instrument of carrying out that wrong. Never was trap more cunningly laid than that in which William now entangled Harold. Never was greater wrong done without the breach of any formal precept of right. William and Lanfranc broke no oath themselves, and that was enough for them. But it was no sin in their eyes to beguile another into engagements which he would understand in one way and they in another; they even, as their admirers tell the story, beguile him into engagements at once unlawful and impossible, because their interests would be promoted by his breach of those engagements. William, in short, under the spiritual guidance of Lanfranc, made Harold swear because he himself would gain by being able to denounce Harold as perjured.

The moral question need not be further discussed; but we should greatly like to know how far the fact of Harold's oath, whatever its nature, was known in England? On this point we have no trustworthy authority. The English writers say nothing about the whole matter; to the Norman writers this point was of no interest. No one mentions this point, except Harold's romantic biographer at the beginning of the thirteenth century. His statements are of no value, except as showing how long Harold's memory was cherished. According to him, Harold formally laid the matter before the Witan, and they unanimously voted that the oath—more, in his version, than a mere oath of homage—was not binding. It is not likely that such a vote was ever formally passed, but its terms would only express what every Englishman would feel. The oath, whatever its terms, had given William a great advantage; but every Englishman would argue both that the oath, whatever its terms, could not hinder the English nation from offering Harold the crown, and that it could not bind Harold to refuse the crown if it should be so offered.

CHAPTER VI—THE NEGOTIATIONS OF DUKE WILLIAM—JANUARY-OCTOBER 1066

If the time that has been suggested was the real time of Harold's oath to William, its fulfilment became a practical question in little more than a year. How the year 1065 passed in Normandy we have no record; in England its later months saw the revolt of Northumberland against Harold's brother Tostig, and the reconciliation which Harold made between the revolters and the king to the damage of his brother's interests. Then came Edward's sickness, of which he died on January 5, 1066. He had on his deathbed recommended Harold to the assembled Witan as his successor in the kingdom. The candidate was at once elected. Whether William, Edgar, or any other, was spoken of we know not; but as to the recommendation of Edward and the consequent election of Harold the English writers are express. The next day Edward was buried, and Harold was crowned in regular form by Ealdred Archbishop of York in Edward's new church at Westminster. Northumberland refused to acknowledge him; but the malcontents were won over by the coming of the king and his friend Saint Wulfstan Bishop of Worcester. It was most likely now, as a seal of this reconciliation, that Harold married Ealdgyth, the sister of the two northern earls Edwin and Morkere, and the widow of the Welsh king Gruffydd. He doubtless hoped in this way to win the loyalty of the earls and their followers.

The accession of Harold was perfectly regular according to English law. In later times endless fables arose; but the Norman writers of the time do not deny the facts of the recommendation, election, and coronation. They slur them over, or, while admitting the mere facts, they represent each act as in some way invalid. No writer near the time asserts a deathbed nomination of William; they speak only of a nomination at some earlier time. But some Norman writers represent Harold as crowned by Stigand Archbishop of Canterbury. This was not, in the ideas of those times, a trifling question. A coronation was then not a mere pageant; it was the actual admission to the kingly office. Till his crowning and anointing, the claimant of the crown was like a bishop-elect before his consecration. He had, by birth or election, the sole right to become king; it was the coronation that made him king. And as the ceremony took the form of an ecclesiastical sacrament, its validity might seem to depend on the lawful position of the officiating bishop. In England to perform that ceremony was the right and duty of the Archbishop of Canterbury; but the canonical position of Stigand was doubtful. He had been appointed on the flight of Robert; he had received the *pallium*, the badge of arch-episcopal rank, only from the usurping Benedict the Tenth. It was therefore good policy in Harold to be crowned by Ealdred, to whose position there was no objection. This is the only difference of fact between the English and Norman versions at this stage. And the difference is easily explained. At William's coronation the king walked to the altar between the two archbishops, but it was Ealdred who actually performed the ceremony. Harold's coronation doubtless followed the same order. But if Stigand took any part in that coronation, it was easy to give out that he took that special part on which the validity of the rite depended.

Still, if Harold's accession was perfectly lawful, it was none the less strange and unusual. Except the Danish kings chosen under more or less of compulsion, he was the first king who did not belong to the West-Saxon kingly house. Such a choice could be justified only on the ground that that house contained no qualified candidate. Its only known members were the children of the Ætheling Edward, young Edgar and his sisters. Now Edgar would certainly have been passed by in favour of any better qualified member of the kingly house, as his father had been passed by in favour of King Edward. And the same principle would, as things stood, justify passing him by in favour of a qualified candidate not of the kingly house. But Edgar's right to the crown is never spoken of till a generation or two later, when the doctrines of hereditary right had gained much greater strength, and when Henry the Second, great-grandson through his mother of Edgar's sister Margaret, insisted on his descent from the old kings. This distinction is important, because Harold is often called an usurper, as keeping out Edgar the heir by birth. But those who called him an usurper at the time called him so as keeping out William the heir by bequest. William's own election was out of the question. He was no more of the English kingly house than Harold; he was a foreigner and an utter stranger. Had Englishmen been minded to choose a foreigner, they doubtless would have chosen Swegen of Denmark. He had found supporters when Edward was chosen; he was afterwards appealed to to deliver England from William. He was no more of the English kingly house than Harold or William; but he was grandson of a man who had reigned over England, Northumberland might have preferred him to Harold; any part of England would have preferred him to William. In fact any choice that could have been made must have had something strange about it. Edgar himself, the one surviving male of the old stock, besides his youth, was neither born in the land nor the son of a crowned king. Those two qualifications had always been deemed of great moment; an elaborate pedigree went for little; actual royal birth went for a great deal. There was now no son of a king to choose. Had there been even a child who was at once a son of Edward and a sister's son of Harold, he might have reigned with his uncle as his guardian and counsellor. As it was, there was nothing to do but to choose the man who, though not of kingly blood, had ruled England well for thirteen years.

The case thus put seemed plain to every Englishman, at all events to every man in Wessex, East-Anglia, and southern Mercia. But it would not seem so plain in *other* lands. To the greater part of Western Europe William's claim might really seem the better. William himself doubtless thought his own claim the better; he deluded himself as he deluded others. But we are more concerned with William as a statesman; and if it be statesmanship to adapt means to ends, whatever the ends may be, if it be statesmanship to make men believe that the worse cause is the better, then no man ever showed higher statesmanship than William showed in his great pleading before all Western Christendom. It is a sign of the times that it was a pleading before all Western Christendom. Others had claimed crowns; none had taken such pains to convince all mankind that the claim was a good one. Such an appeal to public opinion marks on one side a great advance. It was a great step towards the ideas of International Law and even of European concert. It showed that the days of mere force were over, that the days of subtle diplomacy had begun. Possibly the change was not without its dark side; it may be doubted whether a change from force to fraud is wholly a gain. Still it was an appeal from the mere argument of the sword to something which at least professed to be right and reason. William does not draw the sword till he has convinced himself and everybody else that he is drawing it in a just cause. In that age the appeal naturally took a religious shape. Herein lay its immediate strength; herein lay its weakness as regarded the times to come. William appealed to Emperor, kings, princes, Christian men great and small, in every Christian land. He would persuade all; he would ask help of all. But above all he appealed to the head of Christendom, the Bishop of Rome. William in his own person could afford to do so; where he reigned, in Normandy or in England, there was no fear of Roman encroachments; he was fully minded to be in all causes and over all persons within his dominions supreme. While he lived, no Pope ventured to dispute his right. But by acknowledging the right of the Pope to dispose of crowns, or at least to judge as to the right to crowns, he prepared many days of humiliation for kings in general and specially for his own successors. One man in Western Europe could see further than William, perhaps even further than Lanfranc. The chief counsellor of Pope Alexander the Second was the Archdeacon Hildebrand, the future Gregory the Seventh. If William outwitted the world, Hildebrand outwitted William. William's appeal to the Pope to decide between two claimants for the English crown strengthened Gregory not a little in his daring claim to dispose of the crowns of Rome, of Italy, and of Germany. Still this recognition of Roman claims led more directly to the humiliation of William's successor in his own kingdom. Moreover William's successful attempt to represent his enterprise as a holy war, a crusade before crusades were heard of, did much to suggest and to make ready the way for the real crusades a generation later. It was not till after William's death that Urban preached the crusade, but it was during William's life that Gregory planned it.

The appeal was strangely successful. William convinced, or seemed to convince, all men out of England and Scandinavia that his claim to the English crown was just and holy, and that it was a good work to help him to assert it in arms. He persuaded his own subjects; he certainly did not constrain them. He persuaded some foreign princes to give him actual help, some to join his muster in person; he persuaded all to help him so far as not to hinder their subjects from joining him as volunteers. And all this was done by sheer persuasion, by argument good or bad. In adapting of means to ends, in applying to each class of men that kind of argument which best suited it, the diplomacy, the statesmanship, of William was perfect. Again we ask, How far was it the statesmanship of William, how far of Lanfranc? But a prince need not do everything with his own hands and say everything with his own tongue. It was no small part of the statesmanship of William to find out Lanfranc, to appreciate him and to trust him. And when two subtle brains were at work, more could be done by the two working in partnership than by either working alone.

By what arguments did the Duke of the Normans and the Prior of Bec convince mankind that the worse cause was the better? We must always remember the transitional character of the age. England was in political matters in advance of other Western lands; that is, it lagged behind other

Western lands. It had not gone so far on the downward course. It kept far more than Gaul or even Germany of the old Teutonic institutions, the substance of which later ages have won back under new shapes. Many things were understood in England which are now again understood everywhere, but which were no longer understood in France or in the lands held of the French crown. The popular election of kings comes foremost. Hugh Capet was an elective king as much as Harold; but the French kings had made their crown the most strictly hereditary of all crowns. They avoided any interregnum by having their sons crowned in their lifetime. So with the great fiefs of the crown. The notion of kingship as an office conferred by the nation, of a duchy or county as an office held under the king, was still fully alive in England; in Gaul it was forgotten. Kingdom, duchies, counties, had all become possessions instead of offices, possessions passing by hereditary succession of some kind. But no rule of hereditary succession was universally or generally accepted. To this day the kingdoms of Europe differ as to the question of female succession, and it is but slowly that the doctrine of representation has ousted the more obvious doctrine of nearness of kin. All these points were then utterly unsettled; crowns, save of course that of the Empire, were to pass by hereditary right; only what was hereditary right? At such a time claims would be pressed which would have seemed absurd either earlier or later. To Englishmen, if it seemed strange to elect one who was not of the stock of Cerdic, it seemed much more strange to be called on to accept without election, or to elect as a matter of course, one who was not of the stock of Cerdic and who was a stranger into the bargain. Out of England it would not seem strange when William set forth that Edward, having no direct heirs, had chosen his near kinsman William as his successor. Put by itself, that statement had a plausible sound. The transmission of a crown by bequest belongs to the same range of ideas as its transmission by hereditary right; both assume the crown to be a property and not an office. Edward's nomination of Harold, the election of Harold, the fact that William's kindred to Edward lay outside the royal line of England, the fact that there was, in the person of Edgar, a nearer kinsman within that royal line, could all be slurred over or explained away or even turned to William's profit. Let it be that Edward on his death-bed had recommended Harold, and that the Witan had elected Harold. The recommendation was wrung from a dying man in opposition to an earlier act done when he was able to act freely. The election was brought about by force or fraud; if it was free, it was of no force against William's earlier claim of kindred and bequest. As for Edgar, as few people in England thought of him, still fewer out of England would have ever heard of him. It is more strange that the bastardy of William did not tell against him, as it had once told in his own duchy. But this fact again marks the transitional age. Altogether the tale that a man who was no kinsman of the late king had taken to himself the crown which the king had bequeathed to a kinsman, might, even without further aggravation, be easily made to sound like a tale of wrong.

But the case gained tenfold strength when William added that the doer of the wrong was of all men the one most specially bound not to do it. The usurper was in any case William's man, bound to act in all things for his lord. Perhaps he was more; perhaps he had directly sworn to receive William as king. Perhaps he had promised all this with an oath of special solemnity. It would be easy to enlarge on all these further counts as making up an amount of guilt which William not only had the right to chastise, but which he would be lacking in duty if he failed to chastise. He had to punish the perjurer, to avenge the wrongs of the saints. Surely all who should help him in so doing would be helping in a righteous work.

The answer to all this was obvious. Putting the case at the very worst, assuming that Harold had sworn all that he is ever said to have sworn, assuming that he swore it in the most solemn way in which he is ever said to have sworn it, William's claim was not thereby made one whit better. Whatever Harold's own guilt might be, the people of England had no share in it. Nothing that Harold had done could bar their right to choose their king freely. Even if Harold declined the crown, that would not bind the electors to choose William. But when the notion of choosing kings had begun to sound strange, all this would go for nothing. There would be no need even to urge that in any case the wrong done by Harold to William gave William a *casus belli* against Harold, and that William, if victorious, might claim the crown of England, as a possession of Harold's, by right of conquest. In fact William never claimed the crown by conquest, as conquest is commonly understood. He always represented himself as the lawful heir, unhappily driven to use force to obtain his rights. The other pleas were quite enough to satisfy most men out of England and Scandinavia. William's work was to claim the crown of which he was unjustly deprived, and withal to deal out a righteous chastisement on the unrighteous and ungodly man by whom he had been deprived of it.

In the hands of diplomatists like William and Lanfranc, all these arguments, none of which had in itself the slightest strength, were enough to turn the great mass of continental opinion in William's favour. But he could add further arguments specially adapted to different classes of minds. He could hold out the prospect of plunder, the prospect of lands and honours in a land whose wealth was already proverbial. It might of course be answered that the enterprise against England was hazardous and its success unlikely. But in such matters, men listen rather to their hopes than to their fears. To the Normans it would be easy, not only to make out a case against Harold, but to rake up old grudges against the English nation. Under Harold the son of Cnut, Alfred, a prince half Norman by birth, wholly Norman by education, the brother of the late king, the lawful heir to the crown, had been betrayed and murdered by somebody. A widespread belief laid the deed to the charge of the father of the new king. This story might easily be made a ground of national complaint by Normandy against England, and it was easy to infer that Harold had some share in the alleged crime of Godwine. It was easy to dwell on later events, on the driving of so many Normans out of England, with Archbishop Robert at their head. Nay, not only had the lawful primate been driven out, but an usurper had been set in his place, and this usurping archbishop had been made to bestow a mockery of consecration on the usurping king. The proposed aggression on England was even represented as a missionary work, undertaken for the good of the souls of the benighted islanders. For, though the English were undoubtedly devout after their own fashion, there was much in the ecclesiastical state of England which displeased strict churchmen beyond sea, much that William, when he had the power, deemed it his duty to reform. The insular position of England naturally parted it in many things from the usages and feelings of the mainland, and it was not hard to get up a feeling against the nation as well as against its king. All this could not really strengthen William's claim; but it made men look more favourably on his enterprise.

The fact that the Witan were actually in session at Edward's death had made it possible to carry out Harold's election and coronation with extreme speed. The electors had made their choice before William had any opportunity of formally laying his claim before them. This was really an advantage to him; he could the better represent the election and coronation as invalid. His first step was of course to send an embassy to Harold to call on him even now to fulfil his oath. The accounts of this embassy, of which we have no English account, differ as much as the different accounts of the oath. Each version of course makes William demand and Harold refuse whatever it had made Harold swear. These demands and refusals range from the resignation of the kingdom to a marriage with William's daughter. And it is hard to separate this embassy from later messages between the rivals. In all William demands, Harold refuses; the arguments on each side are likely to be genuine. Harold is called on to give up the crown to William, to hold it of William, to hold part of the kingdom of William, to submit the question to the judgement of the Pope, lastly, if he will do nothing else, at least to marry William's daughter. Different writers place these demands at different times, immediately after Harold's election or immediately before the battle. The last challenge to a single combat between Harold and William of course appears only on the eve of the battle. Now none of these accounts come from contemporary partisans of Harold; every one is touched by hostile feeling towards him. Thus the constitutional language that is put into his mouth, almost startling from its modern sound, has greater value. A King of the English can do nothing without the consent of his Witan. They gave him the kingdom; without their consent, he cannot resign it or dismember it or agree to hold it of any man; without their consent, he cannot even marry a foreign wife. Or he answers that the daughter of William whom he promised to marry is dead, and that the sister whom he promised to give to a Norman is dead also. Harold does not deny the fact of his oath—whatever its nature; he justifies its breach because it was taken against is will, and because it was in itself of no strength, as binding him to do impossible things. He does not deny Edward's earlier promise to William; but, as a testament is of no force while the testator liveth, he argues that it is cancelled by Edward's later nomination of himself. In truth there is hardly any difference between the disputants as to matters of fact. One side admits at least a plighting of homage on the part of Harold; the other side admits Harold's nomination and election. The real difference is as to the legal effect of either. Herein comes William's policy. The question was one of English law and of nothing else, a matter for the Witan of England and for no other judges.

William, by ingeniously mixing all kinds of irrelevant issues, contrived to remove the dispute from the region of municipal into that of international law, a law whose chief representative was the Bishop of Rome. By winning the Pope to his side, William could give his aggression the air of a religious war; but in so doing, he unwittingly undermined the throne that he was seeking and the thrones of all other princes.

The answers which Harold either made, or which writers of his time thought that he ought to have made, are of the greatest moment in our constitutional history. The King is the doer of everything; but he can do nothing of moment without the consent of his Witan. They can say Yea or Nay to every proposal of the King. An energetic and popular king would get no answer but Yea to whatever he chose to ask. A king who often got the answer of Nay, Nay, was in great danger of losing his kingdom. The statesmanship of William knew how to turn this constitutional system, without making any change in the letter, into a despotism like that of Constantinople or Cordova. But the letter lived, to come to light again on occasion. The Revolution of 1399 was a falling back on the doctrines of 1066, and the Revolution of 1688 was a falling back on the doctrines of 1399. The principle at all three periods is that the power of the King is strictly limited by law, but that, within the limits which the law sets to his power, he acts according to his own discretion. King and Witan stand out as distinct powers, each of which needs the assent of the other to its acts, and which may always refuse that assent. The political work of the last two hundred years has been to hinder these direct collisions between King and Parliament by the ingenious conventional device of a body of men who shall be in name the ministers of the Crown, but in truth the ministers of one House of Parliament. We do not understand our own political history, still less can we understand the position and the statesmanship of the Conqueror, unless we fully take in what the English constitution in the eleventh century really was, how very modern-sounding are some of its doctrines, some of its forms. Statesmen of our own day might do well to study the meagre records of the Gemót of 1047. There is the earliest recorded instance of a debate on a question of foreign policy. Earl Godwine proposes to give help to Denmark, then at war with Norway. He is outvoted on the motion of Earl Leofric, the man of moderate politics, who appears as leader of the party of non-intervention. It may be that in some things we have not always advanced in the space of eight hundred years.

The negotiations of William with his own subjects, with foreign powers, and with the Pope, are hard to arrange in order. Several negotiations were doubtless going on at the same time. The embassy to Harold would of course come first of all. Till his demand had been made and refused, William could make no appeal elsewhere. We know not whether the embassy was sent before or after Harold's journey to Northumberland, before or after his marriage with Ealdgyth. If Harold was already married, the demand that he should marry William's daughter could have been meant only in mockery. Indeed, the whole embassy was so far meant in mockery that it was sent without any expectation that its demands would be listened to. It was sent to put Harold, from William's point of view, more thoroughly in the wrong, and to strengthen William's case against him. It would therefore be sent at the first moment; the only statement, from a very poor authority certainly, makes the embassy come on the tenth day after Edward's death. Next after the embassy would come William's appeal to his own subjects, though Lanfranc might well be pleading at Rome while William was pleading at Lillebonne. The Duke first consulted a select company, who promised their own services, but declined to pledge any one else. It was held that no Norman was bound to follow the Duke in an attempt to win for himself a crown beyond the sea. But voluntary help was soon ready. A meeting of the whole baronage of Normandy was held at Lillebonne. The assembly declined any obligation which could be turned into a precedent, and passed no general vote at all. But the barons were won over one by one, and each promised help in men and ships according to his means.

William had thus, with some difficulty, gained the support of his own subjects; but when he had once gained it, it was a zealous support. And as the flame spread from one part of Europe to another, the zeal of Normandy would wax keener and keener. The dealings of William with foreign powers are told us in a confused, piecemeal, and sometimes contradictory way. We hear that embassies went to the young King Henry of Germany, son of the great Emperor, the friend of England, and also to Swegen of Denmark. The Norman story runs that both princes promised William their active support. Yet Swegen, the near kinsman of Harold, was a friend of England, and the same writer who puts this promise into his mouth makes him send troops to help his English cousin. Young Henry or his advisers could have no motive for helping William; but subjects of the Empire were at least not hindered from joining his banner. To the French king William perhaps offered the bait of holding the crown of England of him; but Philip is said to have discouraged William's enterprise as much as he could. Still he did not hinder French subjects from taking a part in it. Of the princes who held of the French crown, Eustace of Boulogne, who joined the muster in person, and Guy of Ponthieu, William's own vassal, who sent his son, seem to have been the only ones who did more than allow the levying of volunteers in their dominions. A strange tale is told that Conan of Britanny took this moment for bringing up his own forgotten pretensions to the Norman duchy. If William was going to win England, let him give up Normandy to him. He presently, the tale goes, died of a strange form of poisoning, in which it is implied that William had a hand. This is the story of Walter and Biota over again. It is perhaps enough to say that the Breton writers know nothing of the tale.

But the great negotiation of all was with the Papal court. We might have thought that the envoy would be Lanfranc, so well skilled in Roman ways; but William perhaps needed him as a constant adviser by his own person. Gilbert, Archdeacon of Lisieux, was sent to Pope Alexander. No application could better suit papal interests than the one that was now made; but there were some moral difficulties. Not a few of the cardinals, Hildebrand tells us himself, argued, not without strong language towards Hildebrand, that the Church had nothing to do with such matters, and that it was sinful to encourage a claim which could not be enforced without bloodshed. But with many, with Hildebrand among them, the notion of the Church as a party or a power came before all thoughts of its higher duties. One side was carefully heard; the other seems not to have been heard at all. We hear of no summons to Harold, and the King of the English could not have pleaded at the Pope's bar without acknowledging that his case was at least doubtful. The judgement of Alexander or of Hildebrand was given for William. Harold was declared to be an usurper, perhaps declared excommunicated. The right to the English crown was declared to be in the Duke of the Normans, and William was solemnly blessed in the enterprise in which he was at once to win his own rights, to chastise the wrong-doer, to reform the spiritual state of the misguided islanders, to teach them fuller obedience to the Roman See and more regular payment of its temporal dues. William gained his immediate point; but his successors on the English throne paid the penalty. Hildebrand gained his point for ever, or for as long a time as men might be willing to accept the Bishop of Rome as a judge in any matters. The precedent by which Hildebrand, under another name, took on him to dispose of a higher crown than that of England was now fully established.

As an outward sign of papal favour, William received a consecrated banner and a ring containing a hair of Saint Peter. Here was something for men to fight for. The war was now a holy one. All who were ready to promote their souls' health by slaughter and plunder might flock to William's standard, to the standard of Saint Peter. Men came from most French-speaking lands, the Normans of Apulia and Sicily being of course not slow to take up the quarrel of their kinsfolk. But, next to his own Normandy, the lands which sent most help were Flanders, the land of Matilda, and Britanny, where the name of the Saxon might still be hateful. We must never forget that the host of William, the men who won England, the men who settled in England, were not an exclusively Norman body. Not Norman, but *French*, is the name most commonly opposed to *English*, as the name of the conquering people. Each Norman severally would have scorned that name for himself personally; but it was the only name that could mark the whole of which he and his countrymen formed a part. Yet, if the Normans were but a part, they were the greatest and the noblest part; their presence alone redeemed the enterprise from being a simple enterprise of brigandage. The Norman Conquest was after all a Norman Conquest; men of other lands were merely helpers. So far as it was not Norman, it was Italian; the subtle wit of Lombard Lanfranc and Tuscan Hildebrand did as much to overthrow us as the lance and bow of Normandy.

CHAPTER VII—WILLIAM'S INVASION OF ENGLAND—AUGUST-DECEMBER 1066

The statesmanship of William had triumphed. The people of England had chosen their king, and a large part of the world had been won over by the arts of a foreign prince to believe that it was a righteous and holy work to set him on the throne to which the English people had chosen the foremost man among themselves. No diplomatic success was ever more thorough. Unluckily we know nothing of the state of feeling in England while William was plotting and pleading beyond the sea. Nor do we know how much men in England knew of what was going on in other lands, or what they thought when they heard of it. We know only that, after Harold had won over Northumberland, he came back and held the Easter Gemót at Westminster. Then in the words of the Chronicler, "it was known to him that William Bastard, King Edward's kinsman, would come hither and win this land." This is all that our own writers tell us about William Bastard, between his peaceful visit to England in 1052 and his warlike visit in 1066. But we know that King Harold did all that man could do to defeat his purposes, and that he was therein loyally supported by the great mass of the English nation, we may safely say by all, save his two brothers-in-law and so many as they could influence.

William's doings we know more fully. The military events of this wonderful year there is no need to tell in detail. But we see that William's generalship was equal to his statesmanship, and that it was met by equal generalship on the side of Harold. Moreover, the luck of William is as clear as either his statesmanship or his generalship. When Harold was crowned on the day of the Epiphany, he must have felt sure that he would have to withstand an invasion of England before the year was out. But it could not have come into the mind of Harold, William, or Lanfranc, or any other man, that he would have to withstand two invasions of England at the same moment.

It was the invasion of Harold of Norway, at the same time as the invasion of William, which decided the fate of England. The issue of the struggle might have gone against England, had she had to strive against one enemy only; as it was, it was the attack made by two enemies at once which divided her strength, and enabled the Normans to land without resistance. The two invasions came as nearly as possible at the same moment. Harold Hardrada can hardly have reached the Yorkshire coast before September; the battle of Fulford was fought on September 20th and that of Stamfordbridge on September 25th. William landed on September 28th, and the battle of Senlac was fought on October 14th. Moreover William's fleet was ready by August 12th; his delay in crossing was owing to his waiting for a favourable wind. When William landed, the event of the struggle in the North could not have been known in Sussex. He might have had to strive, not with Harold of England, but with Harold of Norway as his conqueror.

At what time of the year Harold Hardrada first planned his invasion of England is quite uncertain. We can say nothing of his doings till he is actually afloat. And with the three mighty forms of William and the two

Harolds on the scene, there is something at once grotesque and perplexing in the way in which an English traitor flits about among them. The banished Tostig, deprived of his earldom in the autumn of 1065, had then taken refuge in Flanders. He now plays a busy part, the details of which are lost in contradictory accounts. But it is certain that in May 1066 he made an ineffectual attack on England. And this attack was most likely made with the connivance of William. It suited William to use Tostig as an instrument, and to encourage so restless a spirit in annoying the common enemy. It is also certain that Tostig was with the Norwegian fleet in September, and that he died at Stamfordbridge. We know also that he was in Scotland between May and September. It is therefore hard to believe that Tostig had so great a hand in stirring up Harold Hardrada to his expedition as the Norwegian story makes out. Most likely Tostig simply joined the expedition which Harold Hardrada independently planned. One thing is certain, that, when Harold of England was attacked by two enemies at once, it was not by two enemies acting in concert. The interests of William and of Harold of Norway were as much opposed to one another as either of them was to the interests of Harold of England.

One great difficulty beset Harold and William alike. Either in Normandy or in England it was easy to get together an army ready to fight a battle; it was not easy to keep a large body of men under arms for any long time without fighting. It was still harder to keep them at once without fighting and without plundering. What William had done in this way in two invasions of Normandy, he was now called on to do on a greater scale. His great and motley army was kept during a great part of August and September, first at the Dive, then at Saint Valery, waiting for the wind that was to take it to England. And it was kept without doing any serious damage to the lands where they were encamped. In a holy war, this time was of course largely spent in appeals to the religious feelings of the army. Then came the wonderful luck of William, which enabled him to cross at the particular moment when he did cross. A little earlier or later, he would have found his landing stoutly disputed; as it was, he landed without resistance. Harold of England, not being able, in his own words, to be everywhere at once, had done what he could. He and his brothers Gyrth and Leofwine undertook the defence of southern England against the Norman; the earls of the North, his brothers-in-law Edwin and Morkere, were to defend their own land against the Norwegians. His own preparations were looked on with wonder. To guard the long line of coast against the invader, he got together such a force both by sea and land as no king had ever got together before, and he kept it together for a longer time than William did, through four months of inaction, save perhaps some small encounters by sea. At last, early in September, provisions failed; men were no doubt clamouring to go back for the harvest, and the great host had to be disbanded. Could William have sailed as soon as his fleet was ready, he would have found southern England thoroughly prepared to meet him. Meanwhile the northern earls had clearly not kept so good watch as the king. Harold Hardrada harried the Yorkshire coast; he sailed up the Ouse, and landed without resistance. At last the earls met him in arms and were defeated by the Northmen at Fulford near York. Four days later York capitulated, and agreed to receive Harold Hardrada as king. Meanwhile the news reached Harold of England; he got together his housecarls and such other troops as could be mustered at the moment, and by a march of almost incredible speed he was able to save the city and all northern England. The fight of Stamfordbridge, the defeat and death of the most famous warrior of the North, was the last and greatest success of Harold of England. But his northward march had left southern England utterly unprotected. Had the south wind delayed a little longer, he might, before the second enemy came, have been again on the South-Saxon coast. As it was, three days after Stamfordbridge, while Harold of England was still at York, William of Normandy landed without opposition at Pevensey.

Thus wonderfully had an easy path into England been opened for William. The Norwegian invasion had come at the best moment for his purposes, and the result had been what he must have wished. With one Harold he must fight, and to fight with Harold of England was clearly best for his ends. His work would not have been done, if another had stepped in to chastise the perjurer. Now that he was in England, it became a trial of generalship between him and Harold. William's policy was to provoke Harold to fight at once. It was perhaps Harold's policy—so at least thought Gyrth—to follow yet more thoroughly William's own example in the French invasions. Let him watch and follow the enemy, let him avoid all action, and even lay waste the land between London and the south coast, and the strength of the invaders would gradually be worn out. But it might have been hard to enforce such a policy on men whose hearts were stirred by the invasion, and one part of whom, the King's own thegns and housecarls, were eager to follow up their victory over the Northern with a yet mightier victory over the Norman. And Harold spoke as an English king should speak, when he answered that he would never lay waste a single rood of English ground, that he would never harm the lands or the goods of the men who had chosen him to be their king. In the trial of skill between the two commanders, each to some extent carried his point. William's havoc of a large part of Sussex compelled Harold to march at once to give battle. But Harold was able to give battle at a place of his own choosing, thoroughly suited for the kind of warfare which he had to wage.

Harold was blamed, as defeated generals are blamed, for being too eager to fight and not waiting for more troops. But to any one who studies the ground it is plain that Harold needed, not more troops, but to some extent better troops, and that he would not have got those better troops by waiting. From York Harold had marched to London, as the meeting-place for southern and eastern England, as well as for the few who actually followed him from the North and those who joined him on the march. Edwin and Morkere were bidden to follow with the full force of their earldoms. This they took care not to do. Harold and his West-Saxons had saved them, but they would not strike a blow back again. Both now and earlier in the year they doubtless aimed at a division of the kingdom, such as had been twice made within fifty years. Either Harold or William might reign in Wessex and East-Anglia; Edwin should reign in Northumberland and Mercia. William, the enemy of Harold but no enemy of theirs, might be satisfied with the part of England which was under the immediate rule of

Harold and his brothers, and might allow the house of Leofric to keep at least an under-kingship in the North. That the brother earls held back from the King's muster is undoubted, and this explanation fits in with their whole conduct both before and after. Harold had thus at his command the picked men of part of England only, and he had to supply the place of those who were lacking with such forces as he could get. The lack of discipline on the part of these inferior troops lost Harold the battle. But matters would hardly have been mended by waiting for men who had made up their minds not to come.

The messages exchanged between King and Duke immediately before the battle, as well as at an earlier time, have been spoken of already. The challenge to single combat at least comes now. When Harold refused every demand, William called on Harold to spare the blood of his followers, and decide his claims by battle in his own person. Such a challenge was in the spirit of Norman jurisprudence, which in doubtful cases looked for the judgement of God, not, as the English did, by the ordeal, but by the personal combat of the two parties. Yet this challenge too was surely given in the hope that Harold would refuse it, and would thereby put himself, in Norman eyes, yet more thoroughly in the wrong. For the challenge was one which Harold could not but refuse. William looked on himself as one who claimed his own from one who wrongfully kept him out of it. He was plaintiff in a suit in which Harold was defendant; that plaintiff and defendant were both accompanied by armies was an accident for which the defendant, who had refused all peaceful means of settlement, was to blame. But Harold and his people could not look on the matter as a mere question between two men. The crown was Harold's by the gift of the nation, and he could not sever his own cause from the cause of the nation. The crown was his; but it was not his to stake on the issue of a single combat. If Harold were killed, the nation might give the crown to whom they thought good; Harold's death could not make William's claim one jot better. The cause was not personal, but national. The Norman duke had, by a wanton invasion, wronged, not the King only, but every man in England, and every man might claim to help in driving him out. Again, in an ordinary wager of battle, the judgement can be enforced; here, whether William slew Harold or Harold slew William, there was no means of enforcing the judgement except by the strength of the two armies. If Harold fell, the English army were not likely to receive William as king; if William fell, the Norman army was still less likely to go quietly out of England. The challenge was meant as a mere blind; it would raise the spirit of William's followers; it would be something for his poets and chroniclers to record in his honour; that was all.

The actual battle, fought on Senlac, on Saint Calixtus' day, was more than a trial of skill and courage between two captains and two armies. It was, like the old battles of Macedonian and Roman, a trial between two modes of warfare. The English clave to the old Teutonic tactics. They fought on foot in the close array of the shield-wall. Those who rode to the field dismounted when the fight began. They first hurled their javelins, and then took to the weapons of close combat. Among these the Danish axe, brought in by Cnut, had nearly displaced the older English broadsword.

Such was the array of the housecarls and of the thegns who had followed Harold from York or joined him on his march. But the treason of Edwin and Morkere had made it needful to supply the place of the picked men of Northumberland with irregular levies, armed almost anyhow. Of their weapons of various kinds the bow was the rarest. The strength of the Normans lay in the arms in which the English were lacking, in horsemen and archers. These last seem to have been a force of William's training; we first hear of the Norman bowmen at Varaville. These two ways of fighting were brought each one to perfection by the leaders on each side. They had not yet been tried against one another. At Stamfordbridge Harold had defeated an enemy whose tactics were the same as his own. William had not fought a pitched battle since Val-ès-dunes in his youth. Indeed pitched battles, such as English and Scandinavian warriors were used to in the wars of Edmund and Cnut, were rare in continental warfare. That warfare mainly consisted in the attack and defence of strong places, and in skirmishes fought under their walls. But William knew how to make use of troops of different kinds and to adapt them to any emergency. Harold too was a man of resources; he had gained his Welsh successes by adapting his men to the enemy's way of fighting. To withstand the charge of the Norman horsemen, Harold clave to the national tactics, but he chose for the place of battle a spot where those tactics would have the advantage. A battle on the low ground would have been favourable to cavalry; Harold therefore occupied and fenced in a hill, the hill of Senlac, the site in after days of the abbey and town of Battle, and there awaited the Norman attack. The Norman horsemen had thus to make their way up the hill under the shower of the English javelins, and to meet the axes as soon as they reached the barricade. And these tactics were thoroughly successful, till the inferior troops were tempted to come down from the hill and chase the Bretons whom they had driven back. This suggested to William the device of the feigned flight; the English line of defence was broken, and the advantage of ground was lost. Thus was the great battle lost. And the war too was lost by the deaths of Harold and his brothers, which left England without leaders, and by the unyielding valour of Harold's immediate following. They were slain to a man, and south-eastern England was left defenceless.

William, now truly the Conqueror in the vulgar sense, was still far from having full possession of his conquest. He had military possession of part of one shire only; he had to look for further resistance, and he met with not a little. But his combined luck and policy served him well. He could put on the form of full possession before he had the reality; he could treat all further resistance as rebellion against an established authority; he could make resistance desultory and isolated. William had to subdue England in detail; he had never again to fight what the English Chroniclers call a *folk-fight*. His policy after his victory was obvious. Still uncrowned, he was not, even in his own view, king, but he alone had the right to become king. He had thus far been driven to maintain his rights by force; he was not disposed to use force any further, if peaceful possession was to be had. His course was therefore to show himself stern to all who withstood him, but to take all who submitted into his protection and favour. He seems however to have looked for a speedier submission than really happened. He waited a while in his camp for men to come in and acknowledge him. As none came, he set forth to win by the strong arm the land which he claimed of right.

Thus to look for an immediate submission was not unnatural; fully believing in the justice of his own cause, William would believe in it all the more after the issue of the battle. God, Harold had said, should judge between himself and William, and God had judged in William's favour. With all his clear-sightedness, he would hardly understand how differently things looked in English eyes. Some indeed, specially churchmen, specially foreign churchmen, now began to doubt whether to fight against William was not to fight against God. But to the nation at large William was simply as Hubba, Swegen, and Cnut in past times. England had before now been conquered, but never in a single fight. Alfred and Edmund had fought battle after battle with the Dane, and men had no mind to submit to the Norman because he had been once victorious. But Alfred and Edmund, in alternate defeat and victory, lived to fight again; their people had not to choose a new king; the King had merely to gather a new army. But Harold was slain, and the first question was how to fill his place. The Witan, so many as could be got together, met to choose a king, whose first duty would be to meet William the Conqueror in arms. The choice was not easy. Harold's sons were young, and not born Æthelings. His brothers, of whom Gyrth at least must have been fit to reign, had fallen with him. Edwin and Morkere were not at the battle, but they were at the election. But schemes for winning the crown for the house of Leofric would find no favour in an assembly held in London. For lack of any better candidate, the hereditary sentiment prevailed. Young Edgar was chosen. But the bishops, it is said, did not agree; they must have held that God had declared in favour of William. Edwin and Morkere did agree; but they withdrew to their earldoms, still perhaps cherishing hopes of a divided kingdom. Edgar, as king-elect, did at least one act of kingship by confirming the election of an abbot of Peterborough; but of any general preparation for warfare there is not a sign. The local resistance which William met with shows that, with any combined action, the case was not hopeless. But with Edgar for king, with the northern earls withdrawing their forces, with the bishops at least lukewarm, nothing could be done. The Londoners were eager to fight; so doubtless were others; but there was no leader. So far from there being another Harold or Edmund to risk another battle, there was not even a leader to carry out the policy of Fabius and Gyrth.

Meanwhile the Conqueror was advancing, by his own road and after his own fashion. We must remember the effect of the mere slaughter of the great battle. William's own army had suffered severely: he did not leave Hastings till he had received reinforcements from Normandy. But to England the battle meant the loss of the whole force of the south-eastern shires. A large part of England was left helpless. William followed much the same course as he had followed in Maine. A legal claimant of the crown, it was his interest as soon as possible to become a crowned king, and that in his kinsman's church at Westminster. But it was not his interest to march straight on London and demand the crown, sword in hand. He saw that, without the support of the northern earls, Edgar could not possibly stand,

and that submission to himself was only a question of time. He therefore chose a roundabout course through those south-eastern shires which were wholly without means of resisting him. He marched from Sussex into Kent, harrying the land as he went, to frighten the people into submission. The men of Romney had before the battle cut in pieces a party of Normans who had fallen into their hands, most likely by sea. William took some undescribed vengeance for their slaughter. Dover and its castle, the castle which, in some accounts, Harold had sworn to surrender to William, yielded without a blow. Here then he was gracious. When some of his unruly followers set fire to the houses of the town, William made good the losses of their owners. Canterbury submitted; from thence, by a bold stroke, he sent messengers who received the submission of Winchester. He marched on, ravaging as he went, to the immediate neighbourhood of London, but keeping ever on the right bank of the Thames. But a gallant sally of the citizens was repulsed by the Normans, and the suburb of Southwark was burned. William marched along the river to Wallingford. Here he crossed, receiving for the first time the active support of an Englishman of high rank, Wiggod of Wallingford, sheriff of Oxfordshire. He became one of a small class of Englishmen who were received to William's fullest favour, and kept at least as high a position under him as they had held before. William still kept on, marching and harrying, to the north of London, as he had before done to the south. The city was to be isolated within a cordon of wasted lands. His policy succeeded. As no succours came from the North, the hearts of those who had chosen them a king failed at the approach of his rival. At Berkhampstead Edgar himself, with several bishops and chief men, came to make their submission. They offered the crown to William, and, after some debate, he accepted it. But before he came in person, he took means to secure the city. The beginnings of the fortress were now laid which, in the course of William's reign, grew into the mighty Tower of London.

It may seem strange that when his great object was at last within his grasp, William should have made his acceptance of it a matter of debate. He claims the crown as his right; the crown is offered to him; and yet he doubts about taking it. Ought he, he asks, to take the crown of a kingdom of which he has not as yet full possession? At that time the territory of which William had even military possession could not have stretched much to the north-west of a line drawn from Winchester to Norwich. Outside that line men were, as William is made to say, still in rebellion. His scruples were come over by an orator who was neither Norman nor English, but one of his foreign followers, Haimer Viscount of Thouars. The debate was most likely got up at William's bidding, but it was not got up without a motive. William, ever seeking outward legality, seeking to do things peaceably when they could be done peaceably, seeking for means to put every possible enemy in the wrong, wished to make his acceptance of the English crown as formally regular as might be. Strong as he held his claim to be by the gift of Edward, it would be better to be, if not strictly chosen, at least peacefully accepted, by the chief men of England. It might some day serve his purpose to say that the crown had been offered to him, and that he had accepted it only after a debate in which the chief speaker was an impartial stranger.

Having gained this point more, William set out from Berkhampstead, already, in outward form, King-elect of the English.

The rite which was to change him from king-elect into full king took place in Eadward's church of Westminster on Christmas day, 1066, somewhat more than two months after the great battle, somewhat less than twelve months after the death of Edward and the coronation of Harold. Nothing that was needed for a lawful crowning was lacking. The consent of the people, the oath of the king, the anointing by the hands of a lawful metropolitan, all were there. Ealdred acted as the actual celebrant, while Stigand took the second place in the ceremony. But this outward harmony between the nation and its new king was marred by an unhappy accident. Norman horsemen stationed outside the church mistook the shout with which the people accepted the new king for the shout of men who were doing him damage. But instead of going to his help, they began, in true Norman fashion, to set fire to the neighbouring houses. The havoc and plunder that followed disturbed the solemnities of the day and were a bad omen for the new reign. It was no personal fault of William's; in putting himself in the hands of subjects of such new and doubtful loyalty, he needed men near at hand whom he could trust. But then it was his doing that England had to receive a king who needed foreign soldiers to guard him.

William was now lawful King of the English, so far as outward ceremonies could make him so. But he knew well how far he was from having won real kingly authority over the whole kingdom. Hardly a third part of the land was in his obedience. He had still, as he doubtless knew, to win his realm with the edge of the sword. But he could now go forth to further conquests, not as a foreign invader, but as the king of the land, putting down rebellion among his own subjects. If the men of Northumberland should refuse to receive him, he could tell them that he was their lawful king, anointed by their own archbishop. It was sound policy to act as king of the whole land, to exercise a semblance of authority where he had none in fact. And in truth he was king of the whole land, so far as there was no other king. The unconquered parts of the land were in no mood to submit; but they could not agree on any common plan of resistance under any common leader. Some were still for Edgar, some for Harold's sons, some for Swegen of Denmark. Edwin and Morkere doubtless were for themselves. If one common leader could have been found even now, the throne of the foreign king would have been in no small danger. But no such leader came: men stood still, or resisted piecemeal, so the land was conquered piecemeal, and that under cover of being brought under the obedience of its lawful king.

Now that the Norman duke has become an English king, his career as an English statesman strictly begins, and a wonderful career it is. Its main principle was to respect formal legality wherever he could. All William's purposes were to be carried out, as far as possible, under cover of strict adherence to the law of the land of which he had become the lawful ruler. He had sworn at his crowning to keep the laws of the land, and to rule his kingdom as well as any king that had gone before him. And assuredly he meant to keep his oath. But a foreign king, at the head of a foreign army, and who had his foreign followers to reward, could keep that oath only in its letter and not in its spirit. But it is wonderful how nearly he came to keep it in the letter. He contrived to do his most oppressive acts, to deprive Englishmen of their lands and offices, and to part them out among strangers, under cover of English law. He could do this. A smaller man would either have failed to carry out his purposes at all, or he could have carried them out only by reckless violence. When we examine the administration of William more in detail, we shall see that its effects in the long run were rather to preserve than to destroy our ancient institutions. He knew the strength of legal fictions; by legal fictions he conquered and he ruled. But every legal fiction is outward homage to the principle of law, an outward protest against unlawful violence. That England underwent a Norman Conquest did in the end only make her the more truly England. But that this could be was because that conquest was wrought by the Bastard of Falaise and by none other.

CHAPTER VIII—THE CONQUEST OF ENGLAND—DECEMBER 1066-MARCH 1070

The coronation of William had its effect in a moment. It made him really king over part of England; it put him into a new position with regard to the rest. As soon as there was a king, men flocked to swear oaths to him and become his men. They came from shires where he had no real authority. It was most likely now, rather than at Berkhampstead, that Edwin and Morkere at last made up their minds to acknowledge some king. They became William's men and received again their lands and earldoms as his grant. Other chief men from the North also submitted and received their lands and honours again. But Edwin and Morkere were not allowed to go back to their earldoms. William thought it safer to keep them near himself, under the guise of honour—Edwin was even promised one of his daughters in marriage—but really half as prisoners, half as hostages. Of the two other earls, Waltheof son of Siward, who held the shires of Northampton and Huntingdon, and Oswulf who held the earldom of Bernicia or modern Northumberland, we hear nothing at this moment. As for Waltheof, it is strange if he were not at Senlac; it is strange if he were there and came away alive. But we only know that he was in William's allegiance a few months later. Oswulf must have held out in some marked way. It was William's policy to act as king even where he had no means of carrying out his kingly orders. He therefore in February 1067 granted the Bernician earldom to an Englishman named Copsige, who had acted as Tostig's lieutenant. This implies the formal deprivation of Oswulf. But William sent no force with the new earl, who had to take possession as he could. That is to say, of two parties in a local quarrel, one hoped to strengthen itself by making use of William's name. And William thought that it would strengthen his position to let at least his name be heard in every corner of the kingdom. The rest of the story stands rather aloof from the main history. Copsige got possession of the earldom for a moment. He was then killed by Oswulf and his partisans, and Oswulf himself was killed in the course of the year by a common robber. At Christmas, 1067, William again granted or sold the earldom to another of the local chiefs, Gospatric. But he made no attempt to exercise direct authority in those parts till the beginning of the year 1069.

All this illustrates William's general course. Crowned king over the land, he would first strengthen himself in that part of the kingdom which he actually held. Of the passive disobedience of other parts he would take no present notice. In northern and central England William could exercise no authority; but those lands were not in arms against him, nor did they acknowledge any other king. Their earls, now his earls, were his favoured courtiers. He could afford to be satisfied with this nominal kingship, till a fit opportunity came to make it real. He could afford to lend his name to the local enterprise of Copsige. It would at least be another count against the men of Bernicia that they had killed the earl whom King William gave them.

Meanwhile William was taking very practical possession in the shires where late events had given him real authority. His policy was to assert his rights in the strongest form, but to show his mildness and good will by refraining from carrying them out to the uttermost. By right of conquest William claimed nothing. He had come to take his crown, and he had unluckily met with some opposition in taking it. The crown lands of King Edward passed of course to his successor. As for the lands of other men, in William's theory all was forfeited to the crown. The lawful heir had been driven to seek his kingdom in arms; no Englishman had helped him; many Englishmen had fought against him. All then were directly or indirectly traitors. The King might lawfully deal with the lands of all as his own. But in the greater part of the kingdom it was impossible, in no part was it prudent, to carry out this doctrine in its fulness. A passage in Domesday, compared with a passage in the English Chronicles, shows that, soon after William's coronation, the English as a body, within the lands already conquered, redeemed their lands. They bought them back at a price, and held them as a fresh grant from King William. Some special offenders, living and dead, were exempted from this favour. The King took to himself the estates of the house of Godwine, save those of Edith, the widow of his revered predecessor, whom it was his policy to treat with all honour. The lands too of those who had died on Senlac were granted back to their heirs only of special favour, sometimes under the name of alms. Thus, from the beginning of his reign, William began to make himself richer than any king that had been before him in England or than any other Western king of his day. He could both punish his enemies and reward his friends. Much of what he took he kept; much he granted away, mainly to his foreign followers, but sometimes also to Englishmen who had in any way won his favour. Wiggod of Wallingford was one of the very few Englishmen who kept and received estates which put them alongside of the great Norman landowners. The doctrine that all land was held of the King was now put into a practical shape. All, Englishmen and strangers, not only became William's subjects, but his men and his grantees. Thus he went on during his whole reign. There was no sudden change from the old state of things to the new. After the general redemption of lands, gradually carried out as William's power advanced, no general blow was dealt at Englishmen as such. They were not, like some conquered nations, formally degraded or put under any legal incapacities in their own land. William simply distinguished between his loyal and his disloyal subjects, and used his opportunities for punishing the disloyal and rewarding the loyal. Such punishments and rewards naturally took the shape of confiscations and grants of land. If punishment was commonly the lot of the Englishman, and reward was the lot of the stranger, that was only because King William treated all men as they deserved. Most Englishmen were disloyal; most strangers were loyal. But disloyal strangers and loyal Englishmen fared according to their deserts. The final result of this process, begun now and steadily carried on, was that, by the end of William's reign, the foreign king was surrounded by a body of foreign landowners and office-bearers of foreign birth. When, in the early days of his conquest, he gathered round him the great men of his realm, it was still an English assembly with a sprinkling of strangers. By the end of his reign it had changed, step by step, into an assembly of strangers with a sprinkling of Englishmen.

This revolution, which practically transferred the greater part of the soil of England to the hands of strangers, was great indeed. But it must not be mistaken for a sudden blow, for an irregular scramble, for a formal proscription of Englishmen as such. William, according to his character and practice, was able to do all this gradually, according to legal forms, and without drawing any formal distinction between natives and strangers. All land was held of the King of the English, according to the law of England. It may seem strange how such a process of spoliation, veiled under a legal fiction, could have been carried out without resistance. It was easier because it was gradual and piecemeal. The whole country was not touched at once, nor even the whole of any one district. One man lost his land while his neighbour kept his, and he who kept his land was not likely to join in the possible plots of the other. And though the land had never seen so great a confiscation, or one so largely for the behoof of foreigners, yet there was nothing new in the thing itself. Danes had settled under Cnut, and Normans and other Frenchmen under Edward. Confiscation of land was the everyday punishment for various public and private crimes. In any change, such as we should call a change of ministry, as at the fall and the return of Godwine, outlawry and forfeiture of lands was the usual doom of the weaker party, a milder doom than the judicial massacres of later ages. Even a conquest of England was nothing new, and William at this stage contrasted favourably with Cnut, whose early days were marked by the death of not a few. William, at any rate since his crowning, had shed the blood of no man. Men perhaps thought that things might have been much worse, and that they were not unlikely to mend. Anyhow, weakened, cowed, isolated, the people of the conquered shires submitted humbly to the Conqueror's will. It needed a kind of oppression of which William himself was never guilty to stir them into actual revolt.

The provocation was not long in coming. Within three months after his coronation, William paid a visit to his native duchy. The ruler of two states could not be always in either; he owed it to his old subjects to show himself among them in his new character; and his absence might pass as a sign of the trust he put in his new subjects. But the means which he took to secure their obedience brought out his one weak point. We cannot believe that he really wished to goad the people into rebellion; yet the choice of his lieutenants might seem almost like it. He was led astray by partiality for his brother and for his dearest friend. To Bishop Ode of Bayeux, and to William Fitz-Osbern, the son of his early guardian, he gave earldoms, that of Kent to Odo, that of Hereford to William. The Conqueror was determined before all things that his kingdom should be united and obedient; England should not be split up like Gaul and Germany; he would have no man in England whose formal homage should carry with it as little of practical obedience as his own homage to the King of the French. A Norman earl of all Wessex or all Mercia might strive after such a position. William therefore forsook the old practice of dividing the whole kingdom into earldoms. In the peaceful central shires he would himself rule through his sheriffs and other immediate officers; he would appoint earls only in dangerous border districts where they were needed as military commanders. All William's earls were in fact *marquesses*, guardians of a march or frontier. Ode had to keep Kent against attacks from the continent; William Fitz-Osbern had to keep Herefordshire against the Welsh and the independent English. This last shire had its own local warfare. William's authority did not yet reach over all the shires beyond London and Hereford; but Harold had allowed some of Edward's Norman favourites to keep power there. Hereford then and part of its shire formed an isolated part of William's dominions, while the lands around remained unsubdued. William Fitz-Osbern had to guard this dangerous land as earl. But during the King's absence both he and Ode received larger commissions as viceroys over the whole kingdom. Ode guarded the South and William the North and North-East. Norwich, a town dangerous from its easy communication with Denmark, was specially under his care. The nominal earls of the rest of the land, Edwin, Morkere, and Waltheof, with Edgar, King of a moment, Archbishop Stigand, and a number of other chief men, William took with him to Normandy. Nominally his cherished friends and guests, they went in truth, as one of the English Chroniclers calls them, as hostages.

William's stay in Normandy lasted about six months. It was chiefly devoted to rejoicings and religious ceremonies, but partly to Norman legislation. Rich gifts from the spoils of England were given to the churches of Normandy; gifts richer still were sent to the Church of Rome whose favour had wrought so much for William. In exchange for the banner of Saint Peter, Harold's standard of the Fighting-man was sent as an offering to the head of all churches. While William was in Normandy, Archbishop Maurilius of Rouen died. The whole duchy named Lanfranc as his successor; but he declined the post, and was himself sent to Rome to bring the pallium for the new archbishop John, a kinsman of the ducal house. Lanfranc doubtless refused the see of Rouen only because he was designed for a yet greater post in England; the subtlest diplomatist in Europe was not sent to Rome merely to ask for the pallium for Archbishop John.

Meanwhile William's choice of lieutenants bore its fruit in England. They wrought such oppression as William himself never wrought. The inferior leaders did as they thought good, and the two earls restrained them not. The earls meanwhile were in one point there faithfully carrying out the policy of their master in the building of castles; a work, which specially when the work of Ode and William Fitz-Osbern, is always spoken of by the native writers with marked horror. The castles were the badges and the instruments of the Conquest, the special means of holding the land in bondage. Meanwhile tumults broke forth in various parts. The slaughter of Copsige, William's earl in Northumberland, took place about the time of the King's sailing for Normandy. In independent Herefordshire the leading Englishman in those parts, Eadric, whom the Normans called the *Wild*, allied himself with the Welsh, harried the obedient lands, and threatened the castle of Hereford. Nothing was done on either side beyond harrying and skirmishes; but Eadric's corner of the land remained unsubdued. The men of Kent made a strange foreign alliance with Eustace of Boulogne, the brother-in-law of Edward, the man whose deeds had led to the great movement of Edward's reign, to the banishment and the return of Godwine. He had fought against England on Senlac, and was one of four who had dealt the last blow to the wounded Harold. But the oppression of Ode made the Kentishmen glad to seek any help against him. Eustace, now William's enemy, came over, and gave help in an unsuccessful attack on Dover castle. Meanwhile in the obedient shires men were making ready for revolt; in the unsubdued lands they were making ready for more active defence. Many went beyond sea to ask for foreign help, specially in the kindred lands of Denmark and Northern Germany. Against this threatening movement William's strength lay in the incapacity of his enemies for combined action. The whole land never rose at once, and Danish help did not come at the times or in the shape when it could have done most good.

The news of these movements brought William back to England in December. He kept the Midwinter feast and assembly at Westminster; there the absent Eustace was, by a characteristic stroke of policy, arraigned as a traitor. He was a foreign prince against whom the Duke of the Normans might have led a Norman army. But he had also become an English landowner, and in that character he was accountable to the King and Witan of England. He suffered the traitor's punishment of confiscation of lands. Afterwards he contrived to win back William's favour, and he left great English possessions to his second wife and his son. Another stroke of policy was to send an embassy to Denmark, to ward off the hostile purposes of Swegen, and to choose as ambassador an English prelate who had been in high favour with both Edward and Harold, Æthelsige, Abbot of Ramsey. It came perhaps of his mission that Swegen practically did nothing for two years. The envoy's own life was a chequered one. He lost William's favour, and sought shelter in Denmark. He again regained William's favour—perhaps by some service at the Danish court—and died in possession of his abbey.

It is instructive to see how in this same assembly William bestowed several great offices. The earldom of Northumberland was vacant by the slaughter of two earls, the bishopric of Dorchester by the peaceful death of its bishop. William had no real authority in any part of Northumberland, or in more than a small part of the diocese of Dorchester. But he dealt with both earldom and bishopric as in his own power. It was now that he granted Northumberland to Gospatric. The appointment to the bishopric was the beginning of a new system. Englishmen were now to give way step by step to strangers in the highest offices and greatest estates of the land. He had already made two Norman earls, but they were to act as military commanders. He now made an English earl, whose earldom was likely to be either nominal or fatal. The appointment of Remigius of Fécamp to the see of Dorchester was of more real importance. It is the beginning of William's ecclesiastical reign, the first step in William's scheme of making the Church his instrument in keeping down the conquered. While William lived, no Englishman was appointed to a bishopric. As bishoprics became vacant by death, foreigners were nominated, and excuses were often found for hastening a vacancy by deprivation. At the end of William's reign one English bishop only was left. With abbots, as having less temporal power than bishops, the rule was less strict. Foreigners were preferred, but Englishmen were not wholly shut out. And the general process of confiscation and regrant of lands was vigorously carried out. The Kentish revolt and the general movement must have led to many forfeitures and to further grants to loyal men of either nation. As the English Chronicles pithily puts it, "the King gave away every man's land."

William could soon grant lands in new parts of England. In February 1068 he for the first time went forth to warfare with those whom he called his subjects, but who had never submitted to him. In the course of the year a large part of England was in arms against him. But there was no concert; the West rose and the North rose; but the West rose first, and the North did not rise till the West had been subdued. Western England threw off the purely passive state which had lasted through the year 1067. Hitherto each side had left the other alone. But now the men of the West made ready for a more direct opposition to the foreign government. If they could not drive William out of what he had already won, they would at least keep him from coming any further. Exeter, the greatest city of the West, was the natural centre of resistance; the smaller towns, at least of Devonshire and Dorset entered into a league with the capital. They seem to have aimed, like Italian cities in the like case, at the formation of a civic confederation, which might perhaps find it expedient to acknowledge William as an external lord, but which would maintain perfect internal independence. Still, as Gytha, widow of Godwine, mother of Harold, was within the walls of Exeter, the movement was doubtless also in some sort on behalf of the House of Godwine. In any case, Exeter and the lands and towns in its alliance with

Exeter strengthened themselves in every way against attack.

Things were not now as on the day of Senlac, when Englishmen on their own soil withstood one who, however he might cloke his enterprise, was to them simply a foreign invader. But William was not yet, as he was in some later struggles, the *de facto* king of the whole land, whom all had acknowledged, and opposition to whom was in form rebellion. He now held an intermediate position. He was still an invader; for Exeter had never submitted to him; but the crowned King of the English, peacefully ruling over many shires, was hardly a mere invader; resistance to him would have the air of rebellion in the eyes of many besides William and his flatterers. And they could not see, what we plainly see, what William perhaps dimly saw, that it was in the long run better for Exeter, or any other part of England, to share, even in conquest, the fate of the whole land, rather than to keep on a precarious independence to the aggravation of the common bondage. This we feel throughout; William, with whatever motive, is fighting for the unity of England. We therefore cannot seriously regret his successes. But none the less honour is due to the men whom the duty of the moment bade to withstand him. They could not see things as we see them by the light of eight hundred years.

The movement evidently stirred several shires; but it is only of Exeter that we hear any details. William never used force till he had tried negotiation. He sent messengers demanding that the citizens should take oaths to him and receive him within their walls. The choice lay now between unconditional submission and valiant resistance. But the chief men of the city chose a middle course which could gain nothing. They answered as an Italian city might have answered a Swabian Emperor. They would not receive the King within their walls; they would take no oaths to him; but they would pay him the tribute which they had paid to earlier kings. That is, they would not have him as king, but only as overlord over a commonwealth otherwise independent. William's answer was short; "It is not my custom to take subjects on those conditions." He set out on his march; his policy was to overcome the rebellious English by the arms of the loyal English. He called out the *fyrd*, the militia, of all or some of the shires under his obedience. They answered his call; to disobey it would have needed greater courage than to wield the axe on Senlac. This use of English troops became William's custom in all his later wars, in England and on the mainland; but of course he did not trust to English troops only. The plan of the campaign was that which had won Le Mans and London. The towns of Dorset were frightfully harried on the march to the capital of the West. Disunion at once broke out; the leading men in Exeter sent to offer unconditional submission and to give hostages. But the commonalty disowned the agreement; notwithstanding the blinding of one of the hostages before the walls, they defended the city valiantly for eighteen days. It was only when the walls began to crumble away beneath William's mining-engines that the men of Exeter at last submitted to his mercy. And William's mercy could be trusted. No man was harmed in life, limb, or goods. But, to hinder further revolts, a castle was at once begun, and the payments made by the city to the King were largely raised.

Gytha, when the city yielded, withdrew to the Steep Holm, and thence to Flanders. Her grandsons fled to Ireland; from thence, in the course of the same year and the next, they twice landed in Somerset and Devonshire. The Irish Danes who followed them could not be kept back from plunder. Englishmen as well as Normans withstood them, and the hopes of the House of Godwine came to an end.

On the conquest of Exeter followed the submission of the whole West. All the land south of the Thames was now in William's obedience. Gloucestershire seems to have submitted at the same time; the submission of Worcestershire is without date. A vast confiscation of lands followed, most likely by slow degrees. Its most memorable feature is that nearly all Cornwall was granted to William's brother Robert Count of Mortain. His vast estate grew into the famous Cornish earldom and duchy of later times. Southern England was now conquered, and, as the North had not stirred during the stirring of the West, the whole land was outwardly at peace. William now deemed it safe to bring his wife to share his new greatness. The Duchess Matilda came over to England, and was hallowed to Queen at Westminster by Archbishop Ealdred. We may believe that no part of his success gave William truer pleasure. But the presence of the Lady was important in another way. It was doubtless by design that she gave birth on English soil to her youngest son, afterwards the renowned King Henry the First. He alone of William's children was in any sense an Englishman. Born on English ground, son of a crowned King and his Lady, Englishmen looked on him as a countryman. And his father saw the wisdom of encouraging such a feeling. Henry, surnamed in after days the Clerk, was brought up with special care; he was trained in many branches of learning unusual among the princes of his age, among them in a thorough knowledge of the tongue of his native land.

The campaign of Exeter is of all William's English campaigns the richest in political teaching. We see how near the cities of England came for a moment—as we shall presently see a chief city of northern Gaul—to running the same course as the cities of Italy and Provence. Signs of the same tendency may sometimes be suspected elsewhere, but they are not so clearly revealed. William's later campaigns are of the deepest importance in English history; they are far richer in recorded personal actors than the siege of Exeter; but they hardly throw so much light on the character of William and his statesmanship. William is throughout ever ready, but never hasty— always willing to wait when waiting seems the best policy—always ready to accept a nominal success when there is a chance of turning it into a real one, but never accepting nominal success as a cover for defeat, never losing an inch of ground without at once taking measures to recover it. By this means, he has in the former part of 1068 extended his dominion to the Land's End; before the end of the year he extends it to the Tees. In the next year he has indeed to win it back again; but he does win it back and more also. Early in 1070 he was at last, in deed as well as in name, full King over all England.

The North was making ready for war while the war in the West went on, but one part of England did nothing to help the other. In the summer the movement in the North took shape. The nominal earls Edwin, Morkere, and Gospatric, with the Ætheling Edgar and others, left William's court to put themselves at the head of the movement. Edwin was specially aggrieved, because the king had promised him one of his daughters in marriage, but had delayed giving her to him. The English formed alliances with the dependent princes of Wales and Scotland, and stood ready to withstand any attack. William set forth; as he had taken Exeter, he took Warwick, perhaps Leicester. This was enough for Edwin and Morkere. They submitted, and were again received to favour. More valiant spirits withdrew northward, ready to defend Durham as the last shelter of independence, while Edgar and Gospatric fled to the court of Malcolm of Scotland. William went on, receiving the submission of Nottingham and York; thence he turned southward, receiving on his way the submission of Lincoln, Cambridge, and Huntingdon. Again he deemed it his policy to establish his power in the lands which he had already won rather than to jeopard matters by at once pressing farther. In the conquered towns he built castles, and he placed permanent garrisons in each district by granting estates to his Norman and other followers. Different towns and districts suffered in different degrees, according doubtless to the measure of resistance met with in each. Lincoln and Lincolnshire were on the whole favourably treated. An unusual number of Englishmen kept lands and offices in city and shire. At Leicester and Northampton, and in their shires, the wide confiscations and great destruction of houses point to a stout resistance. And though Durham was still untouched, and though William had assuredly no present purpose of attacking Scotland, he found it expedient to receive with all favour a nominal submission brought from the King of Scots by the hands of the Bishop of Durham.

If William's policy ever seems less prudent than usual, it was at the beginning of the next year, 1069. The extreme North still stood out. William had twice commissioned English earls of Northumberland to take possession if they could. He now risked the dangerous step of sending a stranger. Robert of Comines was appointed to the earldom forfeited by the flight of Gospatric. While it was still winter, he went with his force to Durham. By help of the Bishop, he was admitted into the city, but he and his whole force were cut off by the people of Durham and its neighbourhood. Robert's expedition in short led only to a revolt of York, where Edgar was received and siege was laid to the castle. William marched in person with all speed; he relieved the castle; he recovered the city and strengthened it by a second castle on the other side of the river. Still he thought it prudent to take no present steps against Durham. Soon after this came the second attempt of Harold's sons in the West.

Later in this year William's final warfare for the kingdom began. In August, 1069 the long-promised help from Denmark came. Swegen sent his brother Osbeorn and his sons Harold and Cnut, at the head of the whole strength of Denmark and of other Northern lands. If the two enterprises of Harold's sons had been planned in concert with their Danish kinsmen, the invaders or deliverers from opposite sides had failed to act together. Nor are Swegen's own objects quite clear. He sought to deliver England from

William and his Normans, but it is not so plain in whose interest he acted. He would naturally seek the English crown for himself or for one of his sons; the sons of Harold he would rather make earls than kings. But he could feel no interest in the kingship of Edgar. Yet, when the Danish fleet entered the Humber, and the whole force of the North came to meet it, the English host had the heir of Cerdic at its head. It is now that Waltheof the son of Siward, Earl of Northampton and Huntingdon, first stands out as a leading actor. Gospatric too was there; but this time not Edwin and Morkere. Danes and English joined and marched upon York; the city was occupied; the castles were taken; the Norman commanders were made prisoners, but not till they had set fire to the city and burned the greater part of it, along with the metropolitan minster. It is amazing to read that, after breaking down the castles, the English host dispersed, and the Danish fleet withdrew into the Humber.

England was again ruined by lack of concert. The news of the coming of the Danes led only to isolated movements which were put down piecemeal. The men of Somerset and Dorset and the men of Devonshire and Cornwall were put down separately, and the movement in Somerset was largely put down by English troops. The citizens of Exeter, as well as the Norman garrison of the castle, stood a siege on behalf of William. A rising on the Welsh border under Eadric led only to the burning of Shrewsbury; a rising in Staffordshire was held by William to call for his own presence. But he first marched into Lindesey, and drove the crews of the Danish ships across into Holderness; there he left two Norman leaders, one of them his brother Robert of Mortain and Cornwall; he then went westward and subdued Staffordshire, and marched towards York by way of Nottingham. A constrained delay by the Aire gave him an opportunity for negotiation with the Danish leaders. Osbeorn took bribes to forsake the English cause, and William reached and entered York without resistance. He restored the castles and kept his Christmas in the half-burned city. And now William forsook his usual policy of clemency. The Northern shires had been too hard to win. To weaken them, he decreed a merciless harrying of the whole land, the direct effects of which were seen for many years, and which left its mark on English history for ages. Till the growth of modern industry reversed the relative position of Northern and Southern England, the old Northumbrian kingdom never fully recovered from the blow dealt by William, and remained the most backward part of the land. Herein comes one of the most remarkable results of William's coming. His greatest work was to make England a kingdom which no man henceforth thought of dividing. But the circumstances of his conquest of Northern England ruled that for several centuries the unity of England should take the form of a distinct preponderance of Southern England over Northern. William's reign strengthened every tendency that way, chiefly by the fearful blow now dealt to the physical strength and well-being of the Northern shires. From one side indeed the Norman Conquest was truly a Saxon conquest. The King of London and Winchester became more fully than ever king over the whole land.

The Conqueror had now only to gather in what was still left to conquer. But, as military exploits, none are more memorable than the winter marches which put William into full possession of England. The lands beyond Tees still held out; in January 1070 he set forth to subdue them. The Earls Waltheof and Gospatric made their submission, Waltheof in person, Gospatric by proxy. William restored both of them to their earldoms, and received Waltheof to his highest favour, giving him his niece Judith in marriage. But he systematically wasted the land, as he had wasted Yorkshire. He then returned to York, and thence set forth to subdue the last city and shire that held out. A fearful march led him to the one remaining fragment of free England, the unconquered land of Chester. We know not how Chester fell; but the land was not won without fighting, and a frightful harrying was the punishment. In all this we see a distinct stage of moral downfall in the character of the Conqueror. Yet it is thoroughly characteristic. All is calm, deliberate, politic. William will have no more revolts, and he will at any cost make the land incapable of revolt. Yet, as ever, there is no blood shed save in battle. If men died of hunger, that was not William's doing; nay, charitable people like Abbot Æthelwig of Evesham might do what they could to help the sufferers. But the lawful king, kept so long out of his kingdom, would, at whatever price, be king over the whole land. And the great harrying of the northern shires was the price paid for William's kingship over them.

At Chester the work was ended which had begun at Pevensey. Less than three years and a half, with intervals of peace, had made the Norman invader king over all England. He had won the kingdom; he had now to keep it. He had for seventeen years to deal with revolts on both sides of the sea, with revolts both of Englishmen and of his own followers. But in England his power was never shaken; in England he never knew defeat. His English enemies he had subdued; the Danes were allowed to remain and in some sort to help in his work by plundering during the winter. The King now marched to the Salisbury of that day, the deeply fenced hill of Old Sarum. The men who had conquered England were reviewed in the great plain, and received their rewards. Some among them had by failures of duty during the winter marches lost their right to reward. Their punishment was to remain under arms forty days longer than their comrades. William could trust himself to the very mutineers whom he had picked out for punishment. He had now to begin his real reign; and the champion of the Church had before all things to reform the evil customs of the benighted islanders, and to give them shepherds of their souls who might guide them in the right way,

CHAPTER IX—THE SETTLEMENT OF ENGLAND—1070-1086

England was now fully conquered, and William could for a moment sit down quietly to the rule of the kingdom that he had won. The time that immediately followed is spoken of as a time of comparative quiet, and of less oppression than the times either before or after. Before and after, warfare, on one side of the sea or the other, was the main business. Hitherto William has been winning his kingdom in arms. Afterwards he was more constantly called away to his foreign dominions, and his absence always led to greater oppression in England. Just now he had a moment of repose, when he could give his mind to the affairs of Church and State in England. Peace indeed was not quite unbroken. Events were tending to that famous revolt in the Fenland which is perhaps the best remembered part of William's reign. But even this movement was merely local, and did not seriously interfere with William's government. He was now striving to settle the land in peace, and to make his rule as little grievous to the conquered as might be. The harrying of Northumberland showed that he now shrank from no harshness that would serve his ends; but from mere purposeless oppression he was still free. Nor was he ever inclined to needless change or to that scorn of the conquered which meaner conquerors have often shown. He clearly wished both to change and to oppress as little as he could. This is a side of him which has been greatly misunderstood, largely through the book that passes for the History of Ingulf Abbot of Crowland. Ingulf was William's English secretary; a real history of his writing would be most precious. But the book that goes by his name is a forgery not older than the fourteenth century, and is in all points contradicted by the genuine documents of the time. Thus the forger makes William try to abolish the English language and order the use of French in legal writings. This is pure fiction. The truth is that, from the time of William's coming, English goes out of use in legal writings, but only gradually, and not in favour of French. Ever since the coming of Augustine, English and Latin had been alternative tongues; after the coming of William English becomes less usual, and in the course of the twelfth century it goes out of use in favour of Latin. There are no French documents till the thirteenth century, and in that century English begins again. Instead of abolishing the English tongue, William took care that his English-born son should learn it, and he even began to learn it himself. A king of those days held it for his duty to hear and redress his subjects' complaints; he had to go through the land and see for himself that those who acted in his name did right among his people. This earlier kings had done; this William wished to do; but he found his ignorance of English a hindrance. Cares of other kinds checked his English studies, but he may have learned enough to understand the meaning of his own English charters. Nor did William try, as he is often imagined to have done, to root out the ancient institutions of England, and to set up in their stead either the existing institutions of Normandy or some new institutions of his own devising. The truth is that with William began a gradual change in the laws and customs of England, undoubtedly great, but far less than is commonly thought. French names have often supplanted English, and have made the amount of change seem greater than it really was. Still much change did follow on the Norman Conquest, and the Norman Conquest was so completely William's own act that all that came of it was in some sort his act also. But these changes were mainly the gradual results of the state of things which followed William's coming; they were but very slightly the results of any formal acts of his. With a foreign king and foreigners in all high places, much practical change could not fail to follow, even where the letter of the law was unchanged. Still the practical change was less than if the letter of the law had been changed as well. English law was administered by foreign judges; the foreign grantees of William held English land according to English law. The Norman had no special position as a Norman; in every rank except perhaps the very highest and the very lowest, he had Englishmen to his fellows. All this helped to give the Norman Conquest of England its peculiar character, to give it an air of having swept away everything English, while its real work was to turn strangers into Englishmen. And that character was impressed on William's work by William himself. The king claiming by legal right, but driven to assert his right by the sword, was unlike both the foreign king who comes in by peaceful of law. The Normans too, if born soldiers, were also born lawyers, and no man was more deeply impressed with the legal spirit than William himself. He loved neither to change the law nor to transgress the law, and he had little need to do either. He knew how to make the law his instrument, and, without either changing or transgressing it, to use it to make himself all-powerful. He thoroughly enjoyed that system of legal fictions and official euphemisms which marks his reign. William himself became in some sort an Englishman, and those to whom he granted English lands had in some sort to become Englishmen in order to hold them. The Norman stepped into the exact place of the Englishman whose land he held; he took his rights and his burthens, and disputes about those rights and burthens were judged according to English law by the witness of Englishmen. Reigning over two races in one land, William would be lord of both alike, able to use either against the other in case of need. He would make the most of everything in the feelings and customs of either that tended to strengthen his own hands. And, in the state of things in which men then found themselves, whatever strengthened William's hands strengthened law and order in his kingdom.

There was therefore nothing to lead William to make any large changes in the letter of the English law. The powers of a King of the English, wielded as he knew how to wield them, made him as great as he could wish to be. Once granting the original wrong of his coming at all and bringing a host of strangers with him, there is singularly little to blame in the acts of the Conqueror. Of bloodshed, of wanton interference with law and usage, there is wonderfully little. Englishmen and Normans were held to have settled down in peace under the equal protection of King William. The two races were drawing together; the process was beginning which, a hundred years later, made it impossible, in any rank but the highest and the lowest, to distinguish Norman from Englishman. Among the smaller landowners and the townsfolk this intermingling had already begun, while earls and bishops were not yet so exclusively Norman, nor had the free churls of England as yet sunk so low as at a later stage. Still some legislation was needed to settle the relations of the two races. King William proclaimed the "renewal of the law of King Edward." This phrase has often been misunderstood; it is a common form when peace and good order are restored after a period of disturbance. The last reign which is looked back to as to a time of good government becomes the standard of good government, and it is agreed between king and people, between contending races or parties, that things shall be as they were in the days of the model ruler. So we hear in Normandy of the renewal of the law of Rolf, and in England of the renewa of the law of Cnut. So at an earlier time Danes and Englishmen agreed in the renewal of the law of Edgar. So now Normans and Englishmen agreed in the renewal of the law of Edward. There was no code either of Edward's or of William's making. William simply bound himself to rule as Edward had ruled. But in restoring the law of King Edward, he added, "with the additions which I have decreed for the advantage of the people of the English."

These few words are indeed weighty. The little legislation of William's reign takes throughout the shape of additions. Nothing old is repealed; a few new enactments are set up by the side of the old ones. And these words describe, not only William's actual legislation, but the widest general effect of his coming. The Norman Conquest did little towards any direct abolition of the older English laws or institutions. But it set up some new institutions alongside of old ones; and it brought in not a few names, habits, and ways of looking at things, which gradually did their work. In England no man has pulled down; many have added and modified. Our law is still the law of King Edward with the additions of King William. Some old institutions took new names; some new institutions with new names sprang up by the side of old ones. Sometimes the old has lasted, sometimes the new. We still have a *king* and not a *roy*; but he gathers round him a *parliament* and not a *vitenagemót*. We have a *sheriff* and not a *viscount*; but his district is more commonly called a *county* than a *shire*. But *county* and *shire* are French and English for the same thing, and "parliament" is simply French for the "deep speech" which King William had with his Witan. The National Assembly of England has changed its name and its constitution more than once; but it has never been changed by any sudden revolution, never till later times by any formal enactment. There was no moment when one kind of assembly supplanted another. And this has come because our Conqueror was, both by his disposition and his circumstances, led to act as a preserver and not as a destroyer.

The greatest recorded acts of William, administrative and legislative, come in the last days of his reign. But there are several enactments of William belonging to various periods of his reign, and some of them to this first moment of peace. Here we distinctly see William as an English statesman, as a statesman who knew how to work a radical change under conservative forms. One enactment, perhaps the earliest of all, provided for the safety of the strangers who had come with him to subdue and to settle in the land. The murder of a Norman by an Englishman, especially of a Norman intruder by a dispossessed Englishman, was a thing that doubtless often happened. William therefore provides for the safety of those whom he calls "the men whom I brought with me or who have come after me;" that is, the warriors of Senlac, Exeter, and York. These men are put within his own peace; wrong done to them is wrong done to the King, his crown and dignity. If the murderer cannot be found, the lord and, failing him, the hundred, must make payment to the King. Of this grew the presentment of *Englishry*, one of the few formal badges of distinction between the conquering and the conquered race. Its practical need could not have lasted beyond a generation or two, but it went on as a form ages after it had lost all meaning. An unknown corpse, unless it could be proved that the dead man was English, was assumed to be that of a man who had come with King William, and the fine was levied. Some other enactments were needed when two nations lived side by side in the same land. As in earlier times, Roman and barbarian each kept his own law, so now for some purposes the Frenchman—"Francigena"—and the Englishman kept their own law. This is chiefly with regard to the modes of appealing to God's judgement in doubtful cases. The English did this by ordeal, the Normans by wager of battle. When a man of one nation appealed a man of the other, the accused chose the mode of trial. If an Englishman appealed a Frenchman and declined to prove his charge either way, the Frenchman might clear himself by oath. But these privileges were strictly confined to Frenchmen who had come with William and after him. Frenchmen who had in Edward's time settled in England as the land of their own choice, reckoned as Englishmen. Other enactments, fresh enactments of older laws, touched both races. The slave trade was rife in its worst form; men were sold out of the land, chiefly to the Danes of Ireland. Earlier kings had denounced the crime, and earlier bishops had preached against it. William denounced it again under the penalty of forfeiture of all lands and goods, and Saint Wulfstan, the Bishop of Worcester, persuaded the chief offenders, Englishmen of Bristol, to give up their darling sin for a season. Yet in the next reign Anselm and his synod had once more to denounce the crime under spiritual penalties, when they had no longer the strong arm of William to enforce them.

Another law bears more than all the personal impress of William. In it he at once, on one side, forestalls the most humane theories of modern times, and on the other sins most directly against them. His remarkable unwillingness to put any man to death, except among the chances of the battle-field, was to some extent the feeling of his age. With him the feeling takes the shape of a formal law. He forbids the infliction of death for any crime whatever. But those who may on this score be disposed to claim the Conqueror as a sympathizer will be shocked at the next enactment. Those crimes which kings less merciful than William would have punished with death are to be punished with loss of eyes or other foul and cruel mutilations. Punishments of this kind now seem more revolting than death, though possibly, now as then, the sufferer himself might think otherwise. But in those days to substitute mutilation for death, in the case of crimes which were held to deserve death, was universally deemed an act of mercy. Grave men shrank from sending their fellow-creatures out of the world, perhaps without time for repentance; but physical sympathy with physical suffering had little place in their minds. In the next century a feeling against bodily mutilation gradually comes in; but as yet the mildest and most thoughtful men, Anselm himself, make no protest against it when it is believed to be really deserved. There is no sign of any general complaint on this score. The English Chronicler applauds the strict police of which mutilation formed a part, and in one case he deliberately holds it to be the fitting punishment of the offence. In fact, when penal settlements were unknown and legal prisons were few and loathsome, there was something to be said for a punishment which disabled the criminal from repeating his offence. In William's jurisprudence mutilation became the ordinary sentence of the murderer, the robber, the ravisher, sometimes also of English revolters against William's power. We must in short balance his mercy against the mercy of Kirk and Jeffreys.

The ground on which the English Chronicler does raise his wail on behalf of his countrymen is the special jurisprudence of the forests and the extortions of money with which he charges the Conqueror. In both these points the royal hand became far heavier under the Norman rule. In both William's character grew darker as he grew older. He is charged with unlawful exactions of money, in his character alike of sovereign and of landlord. We read of his sharp practice in dealing with the profits of the royal demesnes. He would turn out the tenant to whom he had just let the land, if another offered a higher rent. But with regard to taxation, we must remember that William's exactions, however heavy at the time, were a step in the direction of regular government. In those days all taxation was disliked. Direct taking of the subject's money by the King was deemed an extraordinary resource to be justified only by some extraordinary emergency, to buy off the Danes or to hire soldiers against them. Men long after still dreamed that the King could "live of his own," that he could pay all expenses of his court and government out of the rents and services due to him as a landowner, without asking his people for anything in the character of sovereign. Demands of money on behalf of the King now became both heavier and more frequent. And another change which had long been gradually working now came to a head. When, centuries later, the King was bidden to "live of his own," men had forgotten that the land of the King had once been the land of the nation. In all Teutonic communities, great and small, just as in the city communities of Greece and Italy, the community itself was a chief landowner. The nation had its *folkland*, its *ager publicus*, the property of no one man but of the whole state. Out of this, by the common consent, portions might be cut off and *booked* —granted by a written document—to particular men as their own *bookland*. The King might have his private estate, to be dealt with at his own pleasure, but of the *folkland*, the land of the nation, he was only the chief administrator, bound to act by the advice of his Witan. But in this case more than in others, the advice of the Witan could not fail to become formal; the *folkland*, ever growing through confiscations, ever lessening through grants, gradually came to be looked on as the land of the King, to be dealt with as he thought good. We must not look for any change formally enacted; but in Edward's day the notion of *folkland*, as the possession of the nation and not of the King, could have been only a survival, and in William's day even the survival passed away. The land which was practically the land of King Edward became, as a matter of course, *Terra Regis*, the land of King William. That land was now enlarged by greater confiscations and lessened by greater grants than ever. For a moment, every lay estate had been part of the land of William. And far more than had been the land of the nation remained the land of the King, to be dealt with as he thought good.

In the tenure of land William seems to have made no formal change. But the circumstances of his reign gave increased strength to certain tendencies which had been long afloat. And out of them, in the next reign, the malignant genius of Randolf Flambard devised a systematic code of oppression. Yet even in his work there is little of formal change. There are no laws of William Rufus. The so called feudal incidents, the claims of marriage, wardship, and the like, on the part of the lord, the ancient *heriot* developed into the later *relief,* all these things were in the germ under William, as they had been in the germ long before him. In the hands of Randolf Flambard they stiffen into established custom; their legal acknowledgement comes from the charter of Henry the First which promises to reform their abuses. Thus the Conqueror clearly claimed the right to interfere with the marriages of his nobles, at any rate to forbid a marriage to which he objected on grounds of policy. Under Randolf Flambard this became a regular claim, which of course was made a means of extorting money. Under Henry the claim is regulated and modified, but by being regulated and modified, it is legally established.

The ordinary administration of the kingdom went on under William, greatly modified by the circumstances of his reign, but hardly at all changed in outward form. Like the kings that were before him, he "wore his crown" at the three great feasts, at Easter at Winchester, at Pentecost at Westminster, at Christmas at Gloucester. Like the kings that were before him, he gathered together the great men of the realm, and when need was, the small men also. Nothing seems to have been changed in the constitution or the powers of the assembly; but its spirit must have been utterly changed. The innermost circle, earls, bishops, great officers of state and household, gradually changed from a body of Englishmen with a few strangers among them into a body of strangers among whom two or three Englishmen still kept their places. The result of their "deep speech" with William was not likely to be other than an assent to William's will. The ordinary freeman did not lose his abstract right to come and shout "Yea, yea," to any addition that King William made to the law of King Edward. But there would be nothing to tempt him to come, unless King William thought fit to bid him. But once at least William did gather together, if not every freeman, at least all freeholders of the smallest account. On one point the Conqueror had fully made up his mind; on one point he was to be a benefactor to his kingdom through all succeeding ages. The realm of England was to be one and indivisible. No ruler or subject in the kingdom of England should again dream that that kingdom could be split asunder. When he offered Harold the underkingship of the realm or of some part of it, he did so doubtless only in the full conviction that the offer would be refused. No such offer should be heard of again. There should be no such division as had been between Cnut and Edmund, between Harthacnut and the first Harold, such as Edwin and Morkere had dreamed of in later times. Nor should the kingdom be split asunder in that subtler way which William of all men best understood, the way in which the Frankish kingdoms, East and West, had split asunder. He would have no dukes or earls who might become kings in all but name, each in his own duchy or earldom. No man in his realm should be to him as he was to his overlord at Paris. No man in his realm should plead duty towards an immediate lord as an excuse for breach of duty towards the lord of that immediate lord. Hence William's policy with regard to earldoms. There was to be nothing like the great governments which had been held by Godwine, Leofric, and Siward; an Earl of the West-Saxons or the Northumbrians was too like a Duke of the Normans to be endured by one who was Duke of the Normans himself. The earl, even of the king's appointment, still represented the separate being of the district over which he was set. He was the king's representative rather than merely his officer; if he was a magistrate and not a prince, he often sat in the seat of former princes, and might easily grow into a prince. And at last, at the very end of his reign, as the finishing of his work, he took the final step that made England for ever one. In 1086 every land-owner in England swore to be faithful to King William within and without England and to defend him against his enemies. The subject's duty to the King was to any duty which the vassal might owe to any inferior lord. When the King was the embodiment of national unity and orderly government, this was the greatest of all steps in the direction of both. Never did William or any other man act more distinctly as an English statesman, never did any one act tell more directly towards the later making of England, than this memorable act of the Conqueror. Here indeed is an addition which William made to the law of Edward for the truest good of the English folk. And yet nc enactment has ever been more thoroughly misunderstood. Lawyer after lawyer has set down in his book that, at the assembly of Salisbury in 1086, William introduced "the feudal system." If the words "feudal system" have any meaning, the object of the law now made was to hinder any "feudal system" from coming into England. William would be king of a kingdom, head of a commonwealth, personal lord of every man in his realm, not merely, like a King of the French, external lord of princes whose subjects owed him no allegiance. This greatest monument of the Conqueror's statesmanship was carried into effect in a special assembly of the English nation gathered on the first day of August 1086 on the great plain of Salisbury. Now, perhaps for the first time, we get a distinct foreshadowing of Lords and Commons. The Witan, the great men of the realm, and "the landsitting men," the whole body of landowners, are now distinguished. The point is that William required the personal presence of every man whose personal allegiance he thought worth having. Every man in the mixed assembly, mixed indeed in race and speech, the King's own men and the men of other lords, took the oath and became the man of King William. On that day England became for ever a kingdom one and indivisible, which since that day no man has dreamed of parting asunder.

The great assembly of 1086 will come again among the events of William's later reign; it comes here as the last act of that general settlement which began in 1070. That settlement, besides its secular side, has also an ecclesiastical side of a somewhat different character. In both William's coming brought the island kingdom into a closer connexion with the continent; and brought a large displacement of Englishmen and a large promotion of strangers. But on the ecclesiastical side, though the changes were less violent, there was a more marked beginning of a new state of things. The religious missionary was more inclined to innovate than the military conqueror. Here William not only added but changed; on one point he even proclaimed that the existing law of England was bad. Certainly the religious state of England was likely to displease churchmen from the mainland. The English Church, so directly the child of the Roman, was, for that very reason, less dependent on her parent. She was a free colony, not a conquered province. The English Church too was most distinctly national; no land came so near to that ideal state of things in which the Church is the nation on its religious side. Papal authority therefore was weaker in England than elsewhere, and a less careful line was drawn between spiritual and temporal things and jurisdictions. Two friendly powers could take liberties with each other. The national assemblies dealt with ecclesiastical as well as with temporal matters; one indeed among our ancient laws blames any assembly that did otherwise. Bishop and earl sat together in the local *Gemót*, to deal with many matters which, according to continental ideas, should have been dealt with in separate courts. And, by what in continental eyes seemed a strange laxity of discipline, priests, bishops, members of capitular bodies, were often married. The English diocesan arrangements were unlike continental models. In Gaul, by a tradition of Roman date, the bishop was bishop of the city. His diocese was marked by the extent of the civil jurisdiction of the city. His home, his head church, his *bishopstool* in the head church, were all in the city. In Teutonic England the bishop was commonly bishop, not of a city but of a tribe or district; his style was that of a tribe; his home, his head church, his bishopstool, might be anywhere within the territory of that tribe. Still, on the greatest point of all, matters in England were thoroughly to William's liking; nowhere did the King stand forth more distinctly as the Supreme Governor of the Church. In England, as in Normandy, the right of the sovereign to the investiture of ecclesiastical benefices was ancient and undisputed. What Edward had freely done, William went on freely doing, and Hildebrand himself never ventured on a word of remonstrance against a power which he deemed so wrongful in the hands of his own sovereign. William had but to stand on the rights of his predecessors. When Gregory asked for homage for the crown which he had in some sort given, William answered indeed as an English king. What the kings before him had done for or paid to the Roman see, that would he do and pay; but this no king before him had ever done, nor would he be the first to do it. But while William thus maintained the rights of his crown, he was willing and eager to do all that seemed needful for ecclesiastical reform. And the general result of his reform was to weaken the insular independence of England, to make her Church more like the other Churches of the West, and to increase the power of the Roman Bishop.

William had now a fellow-worker in his taste. The subtle spirit which had helped to win his kingdom was now at his side to help him to rule it. Within a few months after the taking of Chester Lanfranc sat on the throne of Augustine. As soon as the actual Conquest was over, William began to give his mind to ecclesiastical matters. It might look like sacrilege when he caused all the monasteries of England to be harried. But no harm was done to the monks or to their possessions. The holy houses were searched for the hoards which the rich men of England, fearing the new king, had laid up in the monastic treasuries. William looked on these hoards as part of the forfeited goods of rebels, and carried them off during the Lent of 1070. This done, he sat steadily down to the reform of the English Church.

He had three papal legates to guide him, one of whom, Ermenfrid, Bishop of Sitten, had come in on a like errand in the time of Edward. It was a kind of solemn confirmation of the Conquest, when, at the assembly held at Winchester in 1070, the King's crown was placed on his head by Ermenfrid. The work of deposing English prelates and appointing foreign successors now began. The primacy of York was regularly vacant; Ealdred had died as the Danes sailed up the Humber to assault or to deliver his city. The primacy of Canterbury was to be made vacant by the deposition of Stigand. His canonical position had always been doubtful; neither Harold nor William had been crowned by him; yet William had treated him hitherto with marked courtesy, and he had consecrated at least one Norman bishop, Remigius of Dorchester. He was now deprived both of the archbishopric and of the bishopric of Winchester which he held with it, and was kept under restraint for the rest of his life. According to foreign canonical rules the sentence may pass as just; but it marked a stage in the conquest of England when a stout-hearted Englishman was removed from the highest place in the English Church to make way for the innermost counsellor of the Conqueror. In the Pentecostal assembly, held at Windsor, Lanfranc was appointed archbishop; his excuses were overcome by his old master Herlwin of Bec; he came to England, and on August 15, 1070 he was consecrated to the primacy.

Other deprivations and appointments took place in these assemblies. The see of York was given to Thomas, a canon of Bayeux, a man of high character and memorable in the local history of his see. The abbey of Peterborough was vacant by the death of Brand, who had received the staff from the uncrowned Eadgar. It was only by rich gifts that he had turned away the wrath of William from his house. The Fenland was perhaps already stirring, and the Abbot of Peterborough might have to act as a military commander. In this case the prelate appointed, a Norman named Turold, was accordingly more of a soldier than of a monk. From these assemblies of 1070 the series of William's ecclesiastical changes goes on. As the English bishops die or are deprived, strangers take their place. They are commonly Normans, but Walcher, who became Bishop of Durham in 1071, was one of those natives of Lorraine who had been largely favoured in Edward's day. At the time of William's death Wulfstan was the only Englishman who kept a bishopric. Even his deprivation had once been thought of. The story takes a legendary shape, but it throws an important light on the relations of Church and State in England. In an assembly held in the West Minster Wulfstan is called on by William and Lanfranc to give up his staff. He refuses; he will give it back to him who gave it, and places it on the tomb of his dead master Edward. No of his enemies can move it. The sentence is recalled, and the staff yields to his touch. Edward was not yet a canonized saint; the appeal is simply from the living and foreign king to the dead and native king. This legend, growing up when Western Europe was torn in pieces by the struggle about investitures, proves better than the most authentic documents how the right which Popes denied to Emperors was taken for granted in the case of an English king. But, while the spoils of England, temporal and spiritual, were thus scattered abroad among men of the conquering race, two men at least among them refused all share in plunder which they deemed unrighteous. One gallant Norman knight, Gulbert of Hugleville, followed William through all his campaigns, but when English estates were offered as his reward, he refused to share in unrighteous gains, and went back to the lands of his fathers which he could hold with a good conscience. And one monk, Wimund of Saint-Leutfried, not only refused bishoprics and abbeys, but rebuked the Conqueror for wrong and robbery. And William bore no grudge against his censor, but, when the archbishopric of Rouen became vacant, he offered it to the man who had rebuked him. Among the worthies of England Gulbert and Wimund can hardly claim a place, but a place should surely be theirs among the men whom England honours.

The primacy of Lanfranc is one of the most memorable in our history. In the words of the parable put forth by Anselm in the next reign, the plough of the English Church was for seventeen years drawn by two oxen of equal strength. By ancient English custom the Archbishop of Canterbury was the King's special counsellor, the special representative of his Church and people. Lanfranc cannot be charged with any direct oppression; yet in the hands of a stranger who had his spiritual conquest to make, the tribunitian office of former archbishops was lost in that of chief minister o the sovereign. In the first action of their joint rule, the interest of king and primate was the same. Lanfranc sought for a more distinct acknowledgement of the superiority of Canterbury over the rival metropolis of York. And this fell in with William's schemes for the consolidation of the kingdom. The political motive is avowed. Northumberland, which had been so hard to subdue and which still lay open to Danish invaders or deliverers, was still dangerous. An independent Archbishop of York might consecrate a King of the Northumbrians, native or Danish, who might grow into a King of the English. The Northern metropolitan had unwillingly to admit the superiority, and something more, of the Southern. The caution of William and his ecclesiastical adviser reckoned it among possible chances that even Thomas of Bayeux might crown an invading Cnut or Harold in opposition to his native sovereign and benefactor.

For some of his own purposes, William had perhaps chosen his minister too wisely. The objects of the two colleagues were not always the same. Lanfranc, sprung from Imperialist Pavia, was no zealot for extravagant papal claims. The caution with which he bore himself during the schism which followed the strife between Gregory and Henry brought on him more than one papal censure. Yet the general tendency of his administration was towards the growth of ecclesiastical, and even of papal. claims. William never dreamed of giving up his ecclesiastical supremacy or of exempting churchmen from the ordinary power of the law. But the division of the civil and ecclesiastical jurisdiction, the increased frequency of synods distinct from the general assemblies of the realm—even though the acts of those synods needed the royal assent—were steps towards that exemption of churchmen from the civil power which was asserted in one memorable saying towards the end of William's own reign. William could hold his own against Hildebrand himself; yet the increased intercourse with Rome, the more frequent presence of Roman Legates, all tended to increase the papal claims and the deference yielded to them. William refused homage to Gregory; but it is significant that Gregory asked for it. It was a step towards the day when a King of England was glad to offer it. The increased strictness as to the marriage of the clergy tended the same way. Lanfranc did not at once enforce the full rigour of Hildebrand's decrees. Marriage was forbidden for the future; the capitular clergy had to part from their wives; but the vested interest of the parish priest was respected. In another point William directly helped to undermine his own authority and the independence of his kingdom. He exempted his abbey of the Battle from the authority of the diocesan bishop. With this began a crowd of such exemptions, which, by weakening local authority, strengthened the power of the Roman see. All these things helped on Hildebrand's great scheme which made the clergy everywhere members of one distinct and exclusive body, with the Roman Bishop at their head. Whatever tended to part the clergy from other men tended to weaken the throne of every king. While William reigned with Lanfranc at his side, these things were not felt; but the seed was sown for the controversy between Henry and Thomas and for the humiliation of John.

Even those changes of Lanfranc's primacy which seem of purely ecclesiastical concern all helped, in some way to increase the intercourse between England and the continent or to break down some insular peculiarity. And whatever did this increased the power of Rome. Even the decree of 1075 that bishoprics should be removed to the chief cities of their dioceses helped to make England more like Gaul or Italy. So did the fancy of William's bishops and abbots for rebuilding their churches on a greater scale and in the last devised continental style. All tended to make England less of another world. On the other hand, one insular peculiarity well served the purposes of the new primate. Monastic chapters in episcopal churches were almost unknown out of England. Lanfranc, himself a monk, favoured monks in this matter also. In several churches the secular canons were displaced by monks. The corporate spirit of the regulars, and their dependence on Rome, was far stronger than that of the secular clergy. The secular chapters could be refractory, but the disputes between them and their bishops were mainly of local importance; they form no such part of the general story of ecclesiastical and papal advance as the long tale of the quarrel between the archbishops and the monks of Christ Church.

Lanfranc survived William, and placed the crown on the head of his successor. The friendship between king and archbishop remained unbroken through their joint lives. Lanfranc's acts were William's acts; what the Primate did must have been approved by the King. How far William's acts were Lanfranc's acts it is less easy to say. But the Archbishop was ever a trusted minister, and a trusted counsellor, and in the King's frequent absences from England, he often acted as his lieutenant. We do not find him actually taking a part in warfare, but he duly reports military successes to his sovereign. It was William's combined wisdom and good luck to provide himself with a counsellor than whom for his immediate purposes none could be better. A man either of a higher or a lower moral level than Lanfranc, a saint like Anselm or one of the mere worldly bishops of the time, would not have done his work so well. William needed an ecclesiastical statesman, neither unscrupulous nor over-scrupulous, and he found him in the lawyer of Pavia, the doctor of Avranches, the monk of Bec, the abbot of Saint Stephen's. If Lanfranc sometimes unwittingly outwitted both his master and himself, if his policy served the purposes of Rome more than suited the purposes of either, that is the common course of human affairs. Great men are apt to forget that systems which they can work themselves cannot be worked by smaller men. From this error neither William nor Lanfranc was free. But, from their own point of view, it was their only error. Their work was to subdue England, soul and body; and they subdued it. That work could not be done without great wrong: but no other two men of that day could have done it with so little wrong. The shrinking from needless and violent change which is so strongly characteristic of William, and less strongly of Lanfranc also, made their work at the time easier to be done; in the course of ages it made it easier to be undone.

CHAPTER X—THE REVOLTS AGAINST WILLIAM—1070-1086

The years which saw the settlement of England, though not years of constant fighting like the two years between the march to Exeter and the fall of Chester, were not years of perfect peace. William had to withstand foes on both sides of the sea, to withstand foes in his own household, to undergo his first defeat, to receive his first wound in personal conflict. Nothing shook his firm hold either on duchy or kingdom; but in his later years his good luck forsook him. And men did not fail to connect this change in his future with a change in himself, above all with one deed of blood which stands out as utterly unlike all his other recorded acts.

But the amount of warfare which William had to go through in these later years was small compared with the great struggles of his earlier days. There is no tale to tell like the war of Val-ès-dunes, like the French invasions of Normandy, like the campaigns that won England. One event only of the earlier time is repeated almost as exactly as an event can be repeated. William had won Maine once; he had now to win it again, and less thoroughly. As Conqueror his work is done; a single expedition into Wales is the only campaign of this part of his life that led to any increase of territory.

When William sat down to the settlement of his kingdom after the fall of Chester, he was in the strictest sense full king over all England. For the moment the whole land obeyed him; at no later moment did any large part of the land fail to obey him. All opposition was now revolt. Men were no longer keeping out an invader; when they rose, they rose against a power which, however wrongfully, was the established government of the land. Two such movements took place. One was a real revolt of Englishmen against foreign rule. The other was a rebellion of William's own earls in their own interests, in which English feeling went with the King. Both were short sharp struggles which stand out boldly in the tale. More important in the general story, though less striking in detail, are the relations of William to the other powers in and near the isle of Britain. With the crown of the West-Saxon kings, he had taken up their claims to supremacy over the whole island, and probably beyond it. And even without such claims, border warfare with his Welsh and Scottish neighbours could not be avoided. Counting from the completion of the real conquest of England in 1070, there were in William's reign three distinct sources of disturbance. There were revolts within the kingdom of England. There was border warfare in Britain. There were revolts in William's continental dominions. And we may add actual foreign warfare or threats of foreign warfare, affecting William, sometimes in his Norman, sometimes in his English character.

With the affairs of Wales William had little personally to do. In this he is unlike those who came immediately before and after him. In the lives of Harold and of William Rufus personal warfare against the Welsh forms an important part. William the Great commonly left this kind of work to the earls of the frontier, to Hugh of Chester, Roger of Shrewsbury, and to his early friend William of Hereford, so long as that fierce warrior's life lasted. These earls were ever at war with the Welsh princes, and they extended the English kingdom at their cost. Once only did the King take a personal share in the work, when he entered South Wales, in 1081. We hear vaguely of his subduing the land and founding castles; we see more distinctly that he released many subjects who were in British bondage, and that he went on a religious pilgrimage to Saint David's. This last journey is in some accounts connected with schemes for the conquest of Ireland. And in one most remarkable passage of the English Chronicle, the writer for once speculates as to what might have happened but did not. Had William lived two years longer, he would have won Ireland by his wisdom without weapons. And if William had won Ireland either by wisdom or by weapons, he would assuredly have known better how to deal with it than most of those who have come after him. If any man could have joined together the lands which God has put asunder, surely it was he. This mysterious saying must have a reference to some definite act or plan of which we have no other record. And some slight approach to the process of winning Ireland without weapons does appear in the ecclesiastical intercourse between England and Ireland which now begins. Both the native Irish princes and the Danes of the east coast begin to treat Lanfranc as their metropolitan, and to send bishops to him for consecration. The name of the King of the English is never mentioned in the letters which passed between the English primate and the kings and bishops of Ireland. It may be that William was biding his time for some act of special wisdom; but our speculations cannot go any further than those of the Peterborough Chronicler.

Revolt within the kingdom and invasion from without both began in the year in which the Conquest was brought to an end. William's ecclesiastical reforms were interrupted by the revolt of the Fenland. William's authority had never been fully acknowledged in that corner of England, while he wore his crown and held his councils elsewhere. But the place where disturbances began, the abbey of Peterborough, was certainly in William's obedience. The warfare made memorable by the name of Hereward began in June 1070, and a Scottish harrying of Northern England, the second of five which are laid to the charge of Malcolm, took place in the same year, and most likely about the same time. The English movement is connected alike with the course of the Danish fleet and with the appointment of Turold to the abbey of Peterborough. William had bribed the Danish commanders to forsake their English allies, and he allowed them to ravage the coast. A later bribe took them back to Denmark; but not till they had shown themselves in the waters of Ely. The people, largely of Danish descent, flocked to them, thinking, as the Chronicler says, that they would win the whole land. The movement was doubtless in favour of the kingship of Swegen. But nothing was done by Danes and English together save to plunder Peterborough abbey. Hereward, said to have been the nephew of Turold's English predecessor, doubtless looked on the holy place, under a Norman abbot, as part of the enemy's country.

The name of Hereward has gathered round it such a mass of fiction, old and new, that it is hard to disentangle the few details of his real history. His descent and birth-place are uncertain; but he was assuredly a man of Lincolnshire, and assuredly not the son of Earl Leofric. For some unknown cause, he had been banished in the days of Edward or of Harold. He now came back to lead his countrymen against William. He was the soul of the movement of which the abbey of Ely became the centre. The isle, then easily defensible, was the last English ground on which the Conqueror was defied by Englishmen fighting for England. The men of the Fenland were zealous; the monks of Ely were zealous; helpers came in from other parts of England. English leaders left their shelter in Scotland to share the dangers of their countrymen; even Edwin and Morkere at last plucked up heart to leave William's court and join the patriotic movement. Edwin was pursued; he was betrayed by traitors; he was overtaken and slain, to William's deep grief, we are told. His brother reached the isle, and helped in its defence. William now felt that the revolt called for his own presence and his full energies. The isle was stoutly attacked and stoutly defended, till, according to one version, the monks betrayed the stronghold to the King. According to another, Morkere was induced to surrender by promises of mercy which William failed to fulfil. In any case, before the year 1071 was ended, the isle of Ely was in William's hands. Hereward alone with a few companions made their way out by sea. William was less merciful than usual; still no man was put to death. Some were mutilated, some imprisoned; Morkere and other chief men spent the rest of their days in bonds. The temper of the Conqueror had now fearfully hardened. Still he could honour a valiant enemy; those who resisted to the last fared best. All the legends of Hereward's later days speak of him as admitted to William's peace and favour. One makes him die quietly, another kills him at the hands of Norman enemies, but not at William's bidding or with William's knowledge. Evidence a little better suggests that he bore arms for his new sovereign beyond the sea; and an entry in Domesday also suggests that he held lands under Count Robert of Mortain in Warwickshire. It would suit William's policy, when he received Hereward to his favour, to make him exchange lands near to the scene of his exploits for lands in a distant shire held under the lordship of the King's brother.

Meanwhile, most likely in the summer months of 1070, Malcolm ravaged Cleveland, Durham, and other districts where there must have been little left to ravage. Meanwhile the Ætheling Edgar and his sisters, with other English exiles, sought shelter in Scotland, and were hospitably received. At the same time Gospatric, now William's earl in Northumberland, retaliated by a harrying of Scottish Cumberland, which provoked Malcolm to greater cruelties. It was said that there was no house in Scotland so poor that it had not an English bondman. Presently some of Malcolm's English guests joined the defenders of Ely; those of highest birth stayed in Scotland, and Malcolm, after much striving, persuaded Margaret the sister of Edgar to become his wife. Her praises are written in Scottish history, and the marriage had no small share in the process which made the Scottish kings and the lands which formed their real kingdom practically English. The sons and grandsons of Margaret, sprung of the Old-English kingly house, were far more English within their own realm than the Norman and Angevin kings of Southern England. But within the English border men looked at things with other eyes. Thrice again did Malcolm ravage England; two and twenty years later he was slain in his last visit of havoc. William meanwhile and his earls at least drew to themselves some measure of loyalty from the men of Northern England as the guardians of the land against the Scot.

For the present however Malcolm's invasion was only avenged by Gospatric's harrying in Cumberland. The year 1071 called William to Ely; in the early part of 1072 his presence was still needed on the mainland; in August he found leisure for a march against Scotland. He went as an English king, to assert the rights of the English crown, to avenge wrongs done to the English land; and on such an errand Englishmen followed him gladly. Eadric, the defender of Herefordshire, had made his peace with the King, and he now held a place of high honour in his army. But if William met with any armed resistance on his Scottish expedition, it did not amount to a pitched battle. He passed through Lothian into Scotland; he crossed Forth and drew near to Tay, and there, by the round tower of Abernethy, the King of Scots swore oaths and gave hostages and became the man of the King of the English. William might now call himself, like his West-Saxon predecessors, *Bretwalda* and *Basileus* of the isle of Britain. This was the highest point of his fortune. Duke of the Normans, King of the English, he was undisputed lord from the march of Anjou to the narrow sea between Caithness and Orkney.

The exact terms of the treaty between William's royal vassal and his overlord are unknown. But one of them was clearly the removal of Edgar from Scotland. Before long he was on the continent. William had not yet learned that Edgar was less dangerous in Britain than in any other part of the world, and that he was safest of all in William's own court. Homage done and hostages received, the Lord of all Britain returned to his immediate kingdom. His march is connected with many legendary stories. In real history it is marked by the foundation of the castle of Durham, and by the Conqueror's confirmation of the privileges of the palatine bishops. If all the earls of England had been like the earls of Chester, and all the bishops like the bishops of Durham, England would assuredly have split up, like Germany, into a loose federation of temporal and spiritual princes. This it was William's special work to hinder; but he doubtless saw that the exceptional privileges of one or two favoured lordships, standing in marked contrast to the rest, would not really interfere with his great plan of union. And William would hardly have confirmed the sees of London or Winchester in the privileges which he allowed to the distant see of Durham. He now also made a grant of earldoms, the object of which is less clear than that of most of his actions. It is not easy to say why Gospatric was deprived of his earldom. His former acts of hostility to William had been covered by his pardon and reappointment in 1069; and since then he had acted as a loyal, if perhaps an indiscreet, guardian of the land. Two greater earldoms than his had become vacant by the revolt, the death, the imprisonment, of Edwin and Morkere. But these William had no intention of filling. He would not have in his realm anything so dangerous as an earl of the Mercian's or the Northumbrians in the old sense, whether English or Norman. But the defence of the northern frontier needed an earl to rule Northumberland in the later sense, the land north of the Tyne. And after the fate of Robert of Comines, William could not as yet put a Norman earl in so perilous a post. But the Englishman whom he chose was open to the same charges as the deposed Gospatric. For he was Waltheof the son of Siward, the hero of the storm of York in 1069. Already Earl of Northampton and Huntingdon, he was at this time high in the King's personal favour, perhaps already the husband of the King's niece. One side of William's policy comes out here. Union was sometimes helped by division. There were men whom William loved to make great, but whom he had no mind to make dangerous. He gave them vast estates, but estates for the most part scattered over different parts of the kingdom. It was only in the border earldoms and in Cornwall that he allowed anything at all near to the lordship of a whole shire to be put in the hands of a single man. One Norman and one Englishman held two earldoms together; but they were earldoms far apart. Roger of Montgomery held the earldoms of Shrewsbury and Sussex, and Waltheof to his midland earldom of Northampton and Huntingdon now added the rule of distant Northumberland. The men who had fought most stoutly against William were the men whom he most willingly received to favour. Eadric and Hereward were honoured; Waltheof was honoured more highly. He ranked along with the greatest Normans; his position was perhaps higher than any but the King's born kinsmen. But the whole tale of Waltheof is a problem that touches the character of the king under whom he rose and fell. Lifted up higher than any other man among the conquered, he was the one man whom William put to death on a political charge. It is hard to see the reasons for either his rise or his fall. It was doubtless mainly his end which won him the abiding reverence of his countrymen. His valour and his piety are loudly praised. But his valour we know only from his one personal exploit at York; his piety was consistent with a base murder. In other matters, he seems amiable, irresolute, and of a scrupulous conscience, and Northumbrian morality perhaps saw no great crime in a murder committed under the traditions of a Northumbrian deadly feud. Long before Waltheof was born, his grandfather Earl Ealdred had been killed by a certain Carl. The sons of Carl had fought by his side at York; but, notwithstanding this comradeship, the first act of Waltheof's rule in Northumberland was to send men to slay them beyond the bounds of his earldom. A crime that was perhaps admired in Northumberland and unheard of elsewhere did not lose him either the favour of the King or the friendship of his neighbour Bishop Walcher, a reforming prelate with whom Waltheof acted in concert. And when he was chosen as the single exception to William's merciful rule, it was not for this undoubted crime, but on charges of which, even if guilty, he might well have been forgiven.

The sojourn of William on the continent in 1072 carries us out of England and Normandy into the general affairs of Europe. Signs may have already showed themselves of what was coming to the south of Normandy; but the interest of the moment lay in the country of Matilda. Flanders, long the firm ally of Normandy, was now to change into a bitter enemy. Count Baldwin died in 1067; his successor of the same name died three years later, and a war followed between his widow Richildis, the guardian of his young son Arnulf, and his brother Robert the Frisian. Robert had won fame in the East; he had received the sovereignty of Friesland—a name which takes in Holland and Zealand—and he was now invited to deliver Flanders from the oppressions of Richildis. Meanwhile, Matilda was acting as regent of Normandy, with Earl William of Hereford as her counsellor. Richildis sought help of her son's two overlords, King Henry of Germany and King Philip of France. Philip came in person; the German succours were too late. From Normandy came Earl William with a small party of knights. The kings had been asked for armies; to the Earl she offered herself, and he came to fight for his bride. But early in 1071 Philip, Arnulf, and William, were all overthrown by Robert the Frisian in the battle of Cassel. Arnulf and Earl William were killed; Philip made peace with Robert, henceforth undisputed Count of Flanders.

All this brought King William to the continent, while the invasion of Malcolm was still unavenged. No open war followed between Normandy and Flanders; but for the rest of their lives Robert and William were enemies, and each helped the enemies of the other. William gave his support to Baldwin brother of the slain Arnulf, who strove to win Flanders from Robert. But the real interest of this episode lies in the impression which was made in the lands east of Flanders. In the troubled state of Germany, when Henry the Fourth was striving with the Saxons, both sides seem to have looked to the Conqueror of England with hope and with fear.

On this matter our English and Norman authorities are silent, and the notices in the contemporary German writers are strangely unlike one another. But they show at least that the prince who ruled on both sides of the sea was largely in men's thoughts. The Saxon enemy of Henry describes him in his despair as seeking help in Denmark, France, Aquitaine, and also of the King of the English, promising him the like help, if he should ever need it. William and Henry had both to guard against Saxon enmity, but the throne at Winchester stood firmer than the throne at Goslar. But the historian of the continental Saxons puts into William's mouth an answer utterly unsuited to his position. He is made, when in Normandy, to answer that, having won his kingdom by force, he fears to leave it, lest he might not find his way back again. Far more striking is the story told three years later by Lambert of Herzfeld. Henry, when engaged in an Hungarian war, heard that the famous Archbishop Hanno of Köln had leagued with William *Bostar*—so is his earliest surname written—King of the English, and that a vast army was coming to set the island monarch on the German throne. The host never came; but Henry hastened back to guard his frontier against *barbarians*. By that phrase a Teutonic writer can hardly mean the insular part of William's subjects.

Now assuredly William never cherished, as his successor probably did, so wild a dream as that of a kingly crowning at Aachen, to be followed perhaps by an imperial crowning at Rome. But that such schemes were looked on as a practical danger against which the actual German King had to guard, at least shows the place which the Conqueror of England held in European imagination.

For the three or four years immediately following the surrender of Ely, William's journeys to and fro between his kingdom and his duchy were specially frequent. Matilda seems to have always stayed in Normandy; she is never mentioned in England after the year of her coronation and the birth of her youngest son, and she commonly acted as regent of the duchy. In the course of 1072 we see William in England, in Normandy, again in England, and in Scotland. In 1073 he was called beyond sea by a formidable movement. His great continental conquest had risen against him; Le Mans and all Maine were again independent. City and land chose for them a prince who came by female descent from the stock of their ancient counts. This was Hugh the son of Azo Marquess of Liguria and of Gersendis the sister of the last Count Herbert. The Normans were driven out of Le Mans; Azo came to take possession in the name of his son, but he and the citizens did not long agree. He went back, leaving his wife and son under the guardianship of Geoffrey of Mayenne. Presently the men of Le Mans threw off princely rule altogether and proclaimed the earliest *commune* in Northern Gaul. Here then, as at Exeter, William had to strive against an armed commonwealth, and, as at Exeter, we specially wish to know what were to be the relations between the capital and the county at large. The mass of the people throughout Maine threw themselves zealously into the cause of the commonwealth. But their zeal might not have lasted long, if, according to the usual run of things in such cases, they had simply exchanged the lordship of their hereditary masters for the corporate lordship of the citizens of Le Mans. To the nobles the change was naturally distasteful.

They had to swear to the *commune*, but many of them, Geoffrey for one, had no thought of keeping their oaths. Dissensions arose; Hugh went back to Italy; Geoffrey occupied the castle of Le Mans, and the citizens dislodged him only by the dangerous help of the other prince who claimed the overlordship of Maine, Count Fulk of Anjou.

If Maine was to have a master from outside, the lord of Anjou hardly promised better than the lord of Normandy. But men in despair grasp at anything. The strange thing is that Fulk disappears now from the story; William steps in instead. And it was at least as much in his English as in his Norman character that the Duke and King won back the revolted land. A place in his army was held by English warriors, seemingly under the command of Hereward himself. Men who had fought for freedom in their own land now fought at the bidding of their Conqueror to put down freedom in another land. They went willingly; the English Chronicler describes the campaign with glee, and breaks into verse—or incorporates a contemporary ballad—at the tale of English victory. Few men of that day would see that the cause of Maine was in truth the cause of England. If York and Exeter could not act in concert with one another, still less could either act in concert with Le Mans. Englishmen serving in Maine would fancy that they were avenging their own wrongs by laying waste the lands of any man who spoke the French tongue. On William's part, the employment of Englishmen, the employment of Hereward, was another stroke of policy. It was more fully following out the system which led Englishmen against Exeter, which led Eadric and his comrades into Scotland. For in every English soldier whom William carried into Maine he won a loyal English subject. To men who had fought under his banners beyond the sea he would be no longer the Conqueror but the victorious captain; they would need some very special oppression at home to make them revolt against the chief whose laurels they had helped to win. As our own gleeman tells the tale, they did little beyond harrying the helpless land; but in continental writers we can trace a regular campaign, in which we hear of no battles, but of many sieges. William, as before, subdued the land piecemeal, keeping the city for the last. When he drew near to Le Mans, its defenders surrendered at his summons, to escape fire and slaughter by speedy submission. The new *commune* was abolished, but the Conqueror swore to observe all the ancient rights of the city.

All this time we have heard nothing of Count Fulk. Presently we find him warring against nobles of Maine who had taken William's part, and leaguing with the Bretons against William himself. The King set forth with his whole force, Norman and English; but peace was made by the mediation of an unnamed Roman cardinal, abetted, we are told, by the chief Norman nobles. Success against confederated Anjou and Britanny might be doubtful, with Maine and England wavering in their allegiance, and France, Scotland, and Flanders, possible enemies in the distance. The rights of the Count of Anjou over Maine were formally acknowledged, and William's eldest son Robert did homage to Fulk for the county. Each prince stipulated for the safety and favour of all subjects of the other who had taken his side. Between Normandy and Anjou there was peace during the rest of the days of William; in Maine we shall see yet another revolt, though only a partial one.

William went back to England in 1073. In 1074 he went to the continent for a longer absence. As the time just after the first completion of the Conquest is spoken of as a time when Normans and English were beginning to sit down side by side in peace, so the years which followed the submission of Ely are spoken of as a time of special oppression. This fact is not unconnected with the King's frequent absences from England. Whatever we say of William's own position, he was a check on smaller oppressors. Things were always worse when the eye of the great master was no longer watching. William's one weakness was that of putting overmuch trust in his immediate kinsfolk and friends. Of the two special oppressors, William Fitz-Osbern had thrown away his life in Flanders; but Bishop Ode was still at work, till several years later his king and brother struck him down with a truly righteous blow.

The year 1074, not a year of fighting, was pro-eminently a year of intrigue. William's enemies on the continent strove to turn the representative of the West-Saxon kings to help their ends. Edgar flits to and fro between Scotland and Flanders, and the King of the French tempts him with the offer of a convenient settlement on the march of France, Normandy, and Flanders. Edgar sets forth from Scotland, but is driven back by a storm; Malcolm and Margaret then change their minds, and bid him make his peace with King William. William gladly accepts his submission; an embassy is sent to bring him with all worship to the King in Normandy. He abides for several years in William's court contented and despised, receiving a daily pension and the profits of estates in England of no great extent which the King of a moment held by the grant of a rival who could afford to be magnanimous.

Edgar's after-life showed that he belonged to that class of men who, as a rule slothful and listless, can yet on occasion act with energy, and who act most creditably on behalf of others. But William had no need to fear him, and he was easily turned into a friend and a dependant. Edgar, first of Englishmen by descent, was hardly an Englishman by birth. William had now to deal with the Englishman who stood next to Edgar in dignity and far above him in personal estimation. We have reached the great turning-point in William's reign and character, the black and mysterious tale of the fate of Waltheof. The Earl of Northumberland, Northampton, and Huntingdon, was not the only earl in England of English birth. The earldom of the East-Angles was held by a born Englishman who was more hateful than any stranger. Ralph of Wader was the one Englishman who had fought at William's side against England. He often passes for a native of Britanny, and he certainly held lands and castles in that country; but he was Breton only by the mother's side. For Domesday and the Chronicles show that he was the son of an elder Earl Ralph, who had been *staller* or master of the horse in Edward's days, and who is expressly said to have been born in Norfolk. The unusual name suggests that the elder Ralph was not of English descent. He survived the coming of William, and his son fought on Senlac among the countrymen of his mother. This treason implies an unrecorded banishment in the days of Edward or Harold. Already earl in 1069, he had in that year acted vigorously for William against the Danes. But he now conspired against him along with Roger, the younger son of William Fitz-Osbern, who had succeeded his father in the earldom of Hereford, while his Norman estates had passed to his elder brother William. What grounds of complaint either Ralph or Roger had against William we know not; but that the loyalty of the Earl of Hereford was doubtful throughout the year 1074 appears from several letters of rebuke and counsel sent to him by the Regent Lanfranc. At last the wielder of both swords took to his spiritual arms, and pronounced the Earl excommunicate, till he should submit to the King's mercy and make restitution to the King and to all men whom he had wronged. Roger remained stiff-necked under the Primate's censure, and presently committed an act of direct disobedience. The next year, 1075, he gave his sister Emma in marriage to Earl Ralph. This marriage the King had forbidden, on some unrecorded ground of state policy. Most likely he already suspected both earls, and thought any tie between them dangerous. The notice shows William stepping in to do, as an act of policy, what under his successors became a matter of course, done with the sole object of making money. The *bride-ale*—the name that lurks in the modern shape of *bridal*—was held at Exning in Cambridgeshire; bishops and abbots were guests of the excommunicated Roger; Waltheof was there, and many Breton comrades of Ralph. In their cups they began to plot how they might drive the King out of the kingdom. Charges, both true and false, were brought against William; in a mixed gathering of Normans, English, and Bretons, almost every act of William's life might pass as a wrong done to some part of the company, even though some others of the company were his accomplices. Above all, the two earls Ralph and Roger made a distinct proposal to their fellow-earl Waltheof. King William should be driven out of the land; one of the three should be King; the other two should remain earls, ruling each over a third of the kingdom. Such a scheme might attract earls, but no one else; it would undo William's best and greatest work; it would throw back the growing unity of the kingdom by all the steps that it had taken during several generations.

Now what amount of favour did Waltheof give to these schemes? Weighing the accounts, it would seem that, in the excitement of the bride-ale, he consented to the treason, but that he thought better of it the next morning. He went to Lanfranc, at once regent and ghostly father, and confessed to him whatever he had to confess. The Primate assigned his penitent some ecclesiastical penances; the Regent bade the Earl go into Normandy and tell the whole tale to the King. Waltheof went, with gifts in hand; he told his story and craved forgiveness. William made light of the matter, and kept Waltheof with him, but seemingly not under restraint, till he came back to England.

Meanwhile the other two earls were in open rebellion. Ralph, half Breton by birth and earl of a Danish land, asked help in Britanny and Denmark. Bretons from Britanny and Bretons settled in England flocked to him. King Swegen, now almost at the end of his reign and life, listened to the call of the rebels, and sent a fleet under the command of his son Cnut, the future saint, together with an earl named Hakon. The revolt in England was soon put down, both in East and West. The rebel earls met with no support save from those who were under their immediate influence. The country acted zealously for the King. Lanfranc could report that Earl Ralph and his army were fleeing, and that the King's men, French and English, were chasing them. In another letter he could add, with some strength of language, that the kingdom was cleansed from the filth of the Bretons. At Norwich only the castle was valiantly defended by the newly married Countess Emma. Roger was taken prisoner; Ralph fled to Britanny; their followers were punished with various mutilations, save the defenders of Norwich, who were admitted to terms. The Countess joined her husband in Britanny, and in days to come Ralph did something to redeem so many treasons by dying as an armed pilgrim in the first crusade.

The main point of this story is that the revolt met with no English support whatever. Not only did Bishop Wulfstan march along with his fierce Norman brethren Ode and Geoffrey; the English people everywhere were against the rebels. For this revolt offered no attraction to English feeling; had the undertaking been less hopeless, nothing could have been gained by exchanging the rule of William for that of Ralph or Roger. It might have been different if the Danes had played their part better. The rebellion broke out while William was in Normandy; it was the sailing of the Danish fleet which brought him back to England. But never did enterprise bring less honour on its leaders than this last Danish voyage up the Humber. All that the holy Cnut did was to plunder the minster of Saint Peter at York and to sail away.

His coming however seems to have altogether changed the King's feelings with regard to Waltheof. As yet he had not been dealt with as a prisoner or an enemy. He now came back to England with the King, and William's first act was to imprison both Waltheof and Roger. The imprisonment of Roger, a rebel taken in arms, was a matter of course. As for Waltheof, whatever he had promised at the bride-ale, he had done no disloyal act; he had had no share in the rebellion, and he had told the King all that he knew. But he had listened to traitors, and it might be dangerous to leave him at large when a Danish fleet, led by his old comrade Cnut, was actually afloat. Still what followed is strange indeed, specially strange with William as its chief doer.

At the Midwinter Gemót of 1075-1076 Roger and Waltheof were brought to trial. Ralph was condemned in absence, like Eustace of Boulogne. Roger was sentenced to forfeiture and imprisonment for life. Waltheof made his defence; his sentence was deferred; he was kept at Winchester in a straiter imprisonment than before. At the Pentecostal Gemót of 1076, held at Westminster, his case was again argued, and he was sentenced to death. On the last day of May the last English earl was beheaded on the hills above Winchester.

Such a sentence and execution, strange at any time, is specially strange under William. Whatever Waltheof had done, his offence was lighter than that of Roger; yet Waltheof has the heavier and Roger the lighter punishment. With Scroggs or Jeffreys on the bench, it might have been argued that Waltheof's confession to the King did not, in strictness of law, wipe out the guilt of his original promise to the conspirators; but William the Great did not commonly act after the fashion of Scroggs and Jeffreys. To deprive Waltheof of his earldom might doubtless be prudent; a man who had even listened to traitors might be deemed unfit for such a trust. It might be wise to keep him safe under the King's eye, like Edwin, Morkere, and Edgar. But why should he be picked out for death, when the far more guilty Roger was allowed to live? Why should he be chosen as the one victim of a prince who never before or after, in Normandy or in England, doomed any man to die on a political charge? These are questions hard to answer. It is not enough to say that Waltheof was an Englishman, that it was William's policy gradually to get rid of Englishmen in high places, and that the time was now come to get rid of the last. For such a policy forfeiture, or at most imprisonment, would have been enough. While other Englishmen lost lands, honours, at most liberty, Waltheof alone lost his life by a judicial sentence. It is likely enough that many Normans hungered for the lands and honours of the one Englishman who still held the highest rank in England. Still forfeiture without death might have satisfied even them. But Waltheof was not only earl of three shires; he was husband of the King's near kinswoman. We are told that Judith was the enemy and accuser of her husband. This may have touched William's one weak point. Yet he would hardly have swerved from the practice of his whole life to please the bloody caprice of a niece who longed for the death of her husband. And if Judith longed for Waltheof's death, it was not from a wish to supply his place with another. Legend says that she refused a second husband offered her by the King; it is certain that she remained a widow.

Waltheof's death must thus remain a mystery, an isolated deed of blood unlike anything else in William's life. It seems to have been impolitic; it led to no revolt, but it called forth a new burst of English feeling. Waltheof was deemed the martyr of his people; he received the same popular canonization as more than one English patriot. Signs and wonders were wrought at his tomb at Crowland, till displays of miraculous power which were so inconsistent with loyalty and good order were straitly forbidden. The act itself marks a stage in the downward course of William's character. In itself, the harrying of Northumberland, the very invasion of England, with all the bloodshed that they caused, might be deemed blacker crimes than the unjust death of a single man. But as human nature stands, the less crime needs a worse man to do it. Crime, as ever, led to further crime and was itself the punishment of crime. In the eyes of William's contemporaries the death of Waltheof, the blackest act of William's life, was also its turning-point. From the day of the martyrdom on Saint Giles' hill the magic of William's name and William's arms passed away. Unfailing luck no longer waited on him; after Waltheof's death he never, till his last campaign of all, won a battle or took a town. In this change of William's fortunes the men of his own day saw the judgement of God upon his crime. And in the fact at least they were undoubtedly right. Henceforth, though William's real power abides unshaken, the tale of his warfare is chiefly a tale of petty defeats. The last eleven years of his life would never have won him the name of Conqueror. But in the higher walk of policy and legislation never was his nobler surname more truly deserved. Never did William the

Great show himself so truly great as in these later years.

The death of Waltheof and the popular judgement on it suggest another act of William's which cannot have been far from it in point of time, and about which men spoke in his own day in the same spirit. If the judgement of God came on William for the beheading of Waltheof, it came on him also for the making of the New Forest. As to that forest there is a good deal of ancient exaggeration and a good deal of moderr misconception. The word *forest* is often misunderstood. In its older meaning, a meaning which it still keeps in some parts, a forest has nothing to do with trees. It is a tract of land put outside the common law and subject to a stricter law of its own, and that commonly, probably always, to secure for the King the freer enjoyment of the pleasure of hunting. Such a forest William made in Hampshire; the impression which it made on men's minds at the time is shown by its having kept the name of the New Forest for eight hundred years. There is no reason to think that William laid waste any large tract of specially fruitful country, least of all that he laid waste a land thickly inhabited; for most of the Forest land never can have been such. But it is certain from Domesday and the Chronicle that William did *afforest* a considerable tract of land in Hampshire; he set it apart for the purposes of hunting; he fenced it in by special and cruel laws—stopping indeed short of death—for the protection of his pleasures, and in this process some men lost their lands, and were driven from their homes. Some destruction of houses is here implied; some destruction of churches is not unlikely. The popular belief, which hardly differs from the account of writers one degree later than Domesday and the Chronicle, simply exaggerates the extent of destruction. There was no such wide-spread laying waste as is often supposed, because no such wide-spread laying waste was needed. But whatever was needed for William's purpose was done; and Domesday gives us the record. And the act surely makes, like the death of Waltheof, a downward stage in William's character. The harrying of Northumberland was in itself a far greater crime, and involved far more of human wretchedness. But it is not remembered in the same way, because it has left no such abiding memorial. But here again the lesser crime needed a worse man to do it. The harrying of Northumberland was a crime done with a political object; it was the extreme form of military severity; it was not vulgar robbery done with no higher motive than to secure the fuller enjoyment of a brutal sport. To this level William had now sunk. It was in truth now that hunting in England finally took the character of a mere sport. Hunting was no new thing; in an early state of society it is often a necessary thing. The hunting of Alfred is spoken of as a grave matter of business, as part of his kingly duty. He had to make war on the wild beasts, as he had to make war on the Danes. The hunting of William is simply a sport, not his duty or his business, but merely his pleasure. And to this pleasure, the pleasure of inflicting pain and slaughter, he did not scruple to sacrifice the rights of other men, and to guard his enjoyment by ruthless laws at which even in that rough age men shuddered.

For this crime the men of his day saw the punishment in the strange and frightful deaths of his offspring, two sons and a grandson, on the scene of his crime. One of these himself he saw, the death of his second son Richard, a youth of great promise, whose prolonged life might have saved England from the rule of William Rufus. He died in the Forest, about the year 1081, to the deep grief of his parents. And Domesday contains a touching entry, how William gave back his land to a despoiled Englishman as an offering for Richard's soul.

The forfeiture of three earls, the death of one, threw their honours and estates into the King's hands. Another fresh source of wealth came by the death of the Lady Edith, who had kept her royal rank and her great estates, and who died while the proceedings against Waltheof were going on. It was not now so important for William as it had been in the first years of the Conquest to reward his followers; he could now think of the royal hoard in the first place. Of the estates which now fell in to the Crown large parts were granted out. The house of Bigod, afterwards so renowned as Earls of Norfolk, owe their rise to their forefather's share in the forfeited lands of Earl Ralph. But William kept the greater part to himself; one lordship in Somerset, part of the lands of the Lady, he gave to the church of Saint Peter at Rome. Of the three earldoms, those of Hereford and East-Anglia were not filled up; the later earldoms of those lands have no connexion with the earls of William's day. Waltheof's southern earldoms of Northampton and Huntingdon became the dowry of his daughter Matilda; that of Huntingdon passed to his descendants the Kings of Scots. But Northumberland, close on the Scottish border, still needed an earl; but there is something strange in the choice of Bishop Walcher of Durham. It is possible that this appointment was a concession to English feeling stirred to wrath at the death of Waltheof. The days of English earls were over, and a Norman would have been looked on as Waltheof's murderer. The Lotharingian bishop was a stranger; but he was not a Norman, and he was no oppressor of Englishmen. But he was strangely unfit for the place. Not a fighting bishop like Ode and Geoffrey, he was chiefly devoted to spiritual affairs, specially to the revival of the monastic life, which had died out in Northern England since the Danish invasions. But his weak trust in unworthy favourites, English and foreign, led him to a fearful and memorable end. The Bishop was on terms of close friendship with Ligulf, an Englishman of the highest birth and uncle by marriage to Earl Waltheof. He had kept his estates; but the insolence of his Norman neighbours had caused him to come and live in the city of Durham near his friend the Bishop. His favour with Walcher roused the envy of some of the Bishop's favourites, who presently contrived his death. The Bishop lamented, and rebuked them; but he failed to "do justice," to punish the offenders sternly and speedily. He was therefore believed to be himself guilty of Ligulf's death. One of the most striking and instructive events of the time followed. On May 14, 1080, a full Gemót of the earldom was held at Gateshead to deal with the murder of Ligulf. This was one of those rare occasions when a strong feeling led every man to the assembly. The local Parliament took its ancient shape of an armed crowd, headed by the noblest Englishmen left in the earldom. There was no vote, no debate; the shout was "Short rede good rede, slay ye the Bishop." And to that cry, Walcher himself and his companions, the murderers of Ligulf among them, were slaughtered by the raging multitude who had gathered to avenge him.

The riot in which Walcher died was no real revolt against William's government. Such a local rising against a local wrong might have happened in the like case under Edward or Harold. No government could leave such a deed unpunished; but William's own ideas of justice would have been fully satisfied by the blinding or mutilation of a few ringleaders. But William was in Normandy in the midst of domestic and political cares. He sent his brother Ode to restore order, and his vengeance was frightful. The land was harried; innocent men were mutilated and put to death; others saved their lives by bribes. Earl after earl was set over a land so hard to rule. A certain Alberie was appointed, but he was removed as unfit. The fierce Bishop Geoffrey of Coutances tried his hand and resigned. At the time of William's death the earldom was held by Geoffrey's nephew Robert of Mowbray, a stern and gloomy stranger, but whom Englishmen reckoned among "good men," when he guarded the marches of England against the Scot.

After the death of Waltheof William seems to have stayed in Normandy for several years. His ill luck now began. Before the year 1076 was out, he entered, we know not why, on a Breton campaign. But he was driven from Dol by the combined forces of Britanny and France; Philip was ready to help any enemy of William. The Conqueror had now for the first time suffered defeat in his own person. He made peace with both enemies, promising his daughter Constance to Alan of Britanny. But the marriage did not follow till ten years later. The peace with France, as the English Chronicle says, "held little while;" Philip could not resist the temptation of helping William's eldest son Robert when the reckless young man rebelled against his father. With most of the qualities of an accomplished knight, Robert had few of those which make either a wise ruler or an honest man. A brave soldier, even a skilful captain, he was no general; ready of speech and free of hand, he was lavish rather than bountiful. He did not lack generous and noble feelings; but of a steady course, even in evil, he was incapable. As a ruler, he was no oppressor in his own person; but sloth, carelessness, love of pleasure, incapacity to say No, failure to do justice, caused more wretchedness than the oppression of those tyrants who hinder the oppressions of others. William would not set such an one over any part of his dominions before his time, and it was his policy to keep his children dependent on him. While he enriched his brothers, he did not give the smallest scrap of the spoils of England to his sons. But Robert deemed that he had a right to something greater than private estates. The nobles of Normandy had done homage to him as William's successor; he had done homage to Fulk for Maine, as if he were himself its count. He was now stirred up by evil companions to demand that, if his father would not give him part of his kingdom—the spirit of Edwin and Morkere had crossed the sea—he would at least give him Normandy and Maine. William refused with many pithy sayings. It was not his manner to take off his clothes till he went to bed. Robert now, with a band of discontented young nobles, plunged into border warfare against his father. He then wandered over a large part of Europe, begging and receiving money and squandering all that he got. His mother too sent him money, which led to the first quarrel between William and Matilda after so many years of faithful union. William rebuked his wife for helping his enemy in breach of his orders: she pleaded the mother's love for her first-born. The mother was forgiven, but her messenger, sentenced to loss of eyes, found shelter in a monastery.

At last in 1079 Philip gave Robert a settled dwelling-place in the border-fortress of Gerberoi. The strife between father and son became dangerous. William besieged the castle, to undergo before its walls his second defeat, to receive his first wound, and that at the hands of his own son. Pierced in the hand by the lance of Robert, his horse smitten by an arrow, the Conqueror fell to the ground, and was saved only by an Englishman, Tokig, son of Wiggod of Wallingford, who gave his life for his king. It seems an early softening of the tale which says that Robert dismounted and craved his father's pardon; it seems a later hardening which says that William pronounced a curse on his son. William Rufus too, known as yet only as the dutiful son of his father, was wounded in his defence. The blow was not only grievous to William's feelings as a father; it was a serious military defeat. The two wounded Williams and the rest of the besiegers escaped how they might, and the siege of Gerberoi was raised.

We next find the wise men of Normandy debating how to make peace between father and son. In the course of the year 1080 a peace was patched up, and a more honourable sphere was found for Robert's energies in an expedition into Scotland. In the autumn of the year of Gerberoi Malcolm had made another wasting inroad into Northumberland. With the King absent and Northumberland in confusion through the death of Walcher, this wrong went unavenged till the autumn of 1080. Robert gained no special glory in Scotland; a second quarrel with his father followed, and Robert remained a banished man during the last seven years of William's reign.

In this same year 1080 a synod of the Norman Church was held, the Truce of God again renewed which we heard of years ago. The forms of outrage on which the Truce was meant to put a cheek, and which the strong hand of William had put down more thoroughly than the Truce would do, had clearly begun again during the confusions caused by the rebellion of Robert.

The two next years, 1081-1082, William was in England. His home sorrows were now pressing heavily on him. His eldest son was a rebel and an exile; about this time his second son died in the New Forest; according to one version, his daughter, the betrothed of Edwin, who had never forgotten her English lover, was now promised to the Spanish King Alfonso, and died —in answer to her own prayers—before the marriage was celebrated. And now the partner of William's life was taken from him four years after his one difference with her. On November 3, 1083, Matilda died after a long sickness, to her husband's lasting grief. She was buried in her own church at Caen, and churches in England received gifts from William on behalf of her soul.

The mourner had soon again to play the warrior. Nearly the whole of William's few remaining years were spent in a struggle which in earlier times he would surely have ended in a day. Maine, city and county, did not call for a third conquest; but a single baron of Maine defied William's power, and a single castle of Maine held out against him for three years. Hubert, Viscount of Beaumont and Fresnay, revolted on some slight quarrel. The siege of his castle of Sainte-Susanne went on from the death of Matilda til the last year but one of William's reign. The tale is full of picturesque detail; but William had little personal share in it. The best captains of Normandy tried their strength in vain against this one donjon on its rock. William at last made peace with the subject who was too strong for him. Hubert came to England and received the King's pardon. Practically the pardon was the other way.

Thus for the last eleven years of his life William ceased to be the Conqueror. Engaged only in small enterprises, he was unsuccessful in all. One last success was indeed in store for him; but that was to be purchased with his own life. As he turned away in defeat from this castle and that, as he felt the full bitterness of domestic sorrow, he may have thought, as others thought for him, that the curse of Waltheof, the curse of the New Forest, was ever tracking his steps. If so, his crimes were done in England, and their vengeance came in Normandy. In England there was no further room for his mission as Conqueror; he had no longer foes to overcome. He had an act of justice to do, and he did it. He had his kingdom to guard, and he guarded it. He had to take the great step which should make his kingdom one for ever; and he had, perhaps without fully knowing what he did, to bid the picture of his reign be painted for all time as no reign before or after has been painted.

CHAPTER XI—THE LAST YEARS OF WILLIAM—1081-1087

Of two events of these last years of the Conqueror's reign, events of very different degrees of importance, we have already spoken. The Welsh expedition of William was the only recorded fighting on British ground, and that lay without the bounds of the kingdom of England. William now made Normandy his chief dwelling-place, but he was constantly called over to England. The Welsh campaign proves his presence in England in 1081; he was again in England in 1082, but he went back to Normandy between the two visits. The visit of 1082 was a memorable one; there is no more characteristic act of the Conqueror than the deed which marks it. The cruelty and insolence of his brother Ode, whom he had trusted so much more than he deserved, had passed all bounds. In avenging the death of Walcher he had done deeds such as William never did himself or allowed any other man to do. And now, beguiled by a soothsayer who said that one of his name should be the next Pope, he dreamed of succeeding to the throne of Gregory the Seventh. He made all kinds of preparations to secure his succession, and he was at last about to set forth for Italy at the head of something like an army. His schemes were by no means to the liking of his brother. William came suddenly over from Normandy, and met Ode in the Isle of Wight. There the King got together as many as he could of the great men of the realm. Before them he arraigned Ode for all his crimes. He had left him as the lieutenant of his kingdom, and he had shown himself the common oppressor of every class of men in the realm. Last of all, he had beguiled the warriors who were needed for the defence of England against the Danes and Irish to follow him on his wild schemes in Italy. How was he to deal with such a brother, William asked of his wise men.

He had to answer himself; no other man dared to speak. William then gave his judgement. The common enemy of the whole realm should not be spared because he was the King's brother. He should be seized and put in ward. As none dared to seize him, the King seized him with his own hands. And now, for the first time in England, we hear words which were often heard again. The bishop stained with blood and sacrilege appealed to the privileges of his order. He was a clerk, a bishop; no man might judge him but the Pope. William, taught, so men said, by Lanfranc, had his answer ready. "I do not seize a clerk or a bishop; I seize my earl whom I set over my kingdom." So the Earl of Kent was carried off to a prison in Normandy, and Pope Gregory himself pleaded in vain for the release of the Bishop of Bayeux.

The mind of William was just now mainly given to the affairs of his island kingdom. In the winter of 1083 he hastened from the death-bed of his wife to the siege of Sainte-Susanne, and thence to the Midwinter Gemót in England. The chief object of the assembly was the specially distasteful one of laying on of a tax. In the course of the next year, six shillings was levied on every hide of land to meet a pressing need. The powers of the North were again threatening; the danger, if it was danger, was greater than when Waltheof smote the Normans in the gate at York. Swegen and his successor Harold were dead. Cnut the Saint reigned in Denmark, the son-in-law of Robert of Flanders. This alliance with William's enemy joined with his remembrance of his own two failures to stir up the Danish king to a yearning for some exploit in England. English exiles were still found to urge him to the enterprise. William's conquest had scattered banished or discontented Englishmen over all Europe. Many had made their way to the Eastern Rome; they had joined the Warangian guard, the surest support of the Imperial throne, and at Dyrrhachion, as on Senlac, the axe of England had met the lance of Normandy in battle. Others had fled to the North; they prayed Cnut to avenge the death of his kinsman Harold and to deliver England from the yoke of men—so an English writer living in Denmark spoke of them—of Roman speech. Thus the Greek at one end of Europe the Norman at the other, still kept on the name of Rome. The fleet of Denmark was joined by the fleet of Flanders; a smaller contingent was promised by the devout and peaceful Olaf of Norway, who himself felt no call to take a share in the work of war.

Against this danger William strengthened himself by the help of the tax that he had just levied. He could hardly have dreamed of defending

England against Danish invaders by English weapons only. But he thought as little of trusting the work to his own Normans. With the money of England he hired a host of mercenaries, horse and foot, from France and Britanny, even from Maine where Hubert was still defying him at Sainte-Susanne. He gathered this force on the mainland, and came back at its head, a force such as England had never before seen; men wondered how the land might feed them all. The King's men, French and English, had to feed them, each man according to the amount of his land. And now William did what Harold had refused to do; he laid waste the whole coast that lay open to attack from Denmark and Flanders. But no Danes, no Flemings, came. Disputes arose between Cnut and his brother Olaf, and the great enterprise came to nothing. William kept part of his mercenaries in England, and part he sent to their homes. Cnut was murdered in a church by his own subjects, and was canonized as *Sanctus Canutus* by a Pope who could not speak the Scandinavian name.

Meanwhile, at the Midwinter Gemót of 1085-1086, held in due form at Gloucester, William did one of his greatest acts. "The King had mickle thought and sooth deep speech with his Witan about his land, how it were set and with whilk men." In that "deep speech," so called in our own tongue, lurks a name well known and dear to every Englishman. The result of that famous parliament is set forth at length by the Chronicler. The King sent his men into each shire, men who did indeed set down in their writ how the land was set and of what men. In that writ we have a record in the Roman tongue no less precious than the Chronicles in our own. For that writ became the Book of Winchester, the book to which our fathers gave the name of Domesday, the book of judgement that spared no man.

The Great Survey was made in the course of the first seven months of the year 1086. Commissioners were sent into every shire, who inquired by the oaths of the men of the hundreds by whom the land had been held in King Edward's days and what it was worth then, by whom it was held at the time of the survey and what it was worth then; and lastly, whether its worth could be raised. Nothing was to be left out. "So sooth narrowly did he let spear it out, that there was not a hide or a yard of land, nor further—it is shame to tell, and it thought him no shame to do—an ox nor a cow nor a swine was left that was not set in his writ." This kind of searching inquiry, never liked at any time, would be specially grievous then. The taking of the survey led to disturbances in many places, in which not a few lives were lost. While the work was going on, William went to and fro till he knew thoroughly how this land was set and of what men. He had now a list of all men, French and English, who held land in his kingdom. And it was not enough to have their names in a writ; he would see them face to face. On the making of the survey followed that great assembly, that great work of legislation, which was the crown of William's life as a ruler and lawgiver of England. The usual assemblies of the year had been held at Winchester and Westminster. An extraordinary assembly was held in the plain of Salisbury on the first day of August. The work of that assembly has been already spoken of. It was now that all the owners of land in the kingdom became the men of the King; it was now that England became one, with no fear of being again parted asunder.

The close connexion between the Great Survey and the law and the oath of Salisbury is plain. It was a great matter for the King to get in the gold certainly and, we may add, fairly. William would deal with no man otherwise than according to law as he understood the law. But he sought for more than this. He would not only know what this land could be made to pay; he would know the state of his kingdom in every detail; he would know its military strength; he would know whether his own will, in the long process of taking from this man and giving to that, had been really carried out. Domesday is before all things a record of the great confiscation, a record of that gradual change by which, in less than twenty years, the greater part of the land of England had been transferred from native to foreign owners. And nothing shows like Domesday in what a formally legal fashion that transfer was carried out. What were the principles on which it was carried out, we have already seen. All private property in land came only from the grant of King William. It had all passed into his hands by lawful forfeiture; he might keep it himself; he might give it back to its old owner or grant it to a new one. So it was at the general redemption of lands; so it was whenever fresh conquests or fresh revolts threw fresh lands into the King's hands. The principle is so thoroughly taken for granted, that we are a little startled to find it incidentally set forth in so many words in a case of no special importance. A priest named Robert held a single yardland in alms of the King; he became a monk in the monastery of Stow-in-Lindesey, and his yardland became the property of the house. One hardly sees why this case should have been picked out for a solemn declaration of the general law. Yet, as "the day on which the English redeemed their lands" is spoken of only casually in the case of a particular estate, so the principle that no man could hold lands except by the King's grant ("Non licet terram alicui habere nisi regis concessu") is brought in only to illustrate the wrongful dealing of Robert and the monks of Stow in the case of a very small holding indeed.

All this is a vast system of legal fictions; for William's whole position, the whole scheme of his government, rested on a system of legal fictions. Domesday is full of them; one might almost say that there is nothing else there. A very attentive study of Domesday might bring out the fact that William was a foreign conqueror, and that the book itself was a record of the process by which he took the lands of the natives who had fought against him to reward the strangers who had fought for him. But nothing of this kind appears on the surface of the record. The great facts of the Conquest are put out of sight. William is taken for granted, not only as the lawful king, but as the immediate successor of Edward. The "time of King Edward" and the "time of King William" are the two times that the law knows of. The compilers of the record are put to some curious shifts to describe the time between "the day when King Edward was alive and dead" and the day "when King William came into England." That coming might have been as peaceful as the coming of James the First or George the First. The two great battles are more than once referred to, but only casually in the mention of particular persons. A very sharp critic might guess that one of them had something to do with King William's coming into England; but that is all. Harold appears only as Earl; it is only in two or three places that we hear of a "time of Harold," and even of Harold "seizing the kingdom" and "reigning." These two or three places stand out in such contrast to the general language of the record that we are led to think that the scribe must have copied some earlier record or taken down the words of some witness, and must have forgotten to translate them into more loyal formulae. So in recording who held the land in King Edward's day and who in King William's, there is nothing to show that in so many cases the holder under Edward had been turned out to make room for the holder under William. The former holder is marked by the perfectly colourless word "ancestor" ("antecessor"), a word as yet meaning, not "forefather," but "predecessor" of any kind. In Domesday the word is most commonly an euphemism for "dispossessed Englishman." It is a still more distinct euphemism where the Norman holder is in more than one place called the "heir" of the dispossessed Englishmen.

The formulae of Domesday are the most speaking witness to the spirit of outward legality which ruled every act of William. In this way they are wonderfully instructive; but from the formulae alone no one could ever make the real facts of William's coming and reign. It is the incidental notices which make us more at home in the local and personal life of this reign than of any reign before or for a long time after. The Commissioners had to report whether the King's will had been everywhere carried out, whether every man, great and small, French and English, had what the King meant him to have, neither more nor less. And they had often to report a state of things different from what the King had meant to be. Many men had not all that King William had meant them to have, and many others had much more. Normans had taken both from Englishmen and from other Normans. Englishmen had taken from Englishmen; some had taken from ecclesiastical bodies; some had taken from King William himself; nay King William himself holds lands which he ought to give up to another man. This last entry at least shows that William was fully ready to do right, according to his notions of right. So also the King's two brothers are set down among the chief offenders. Of these unlawful holdings of land marked in the technical language of the Survey as *invasiones* and *occupationes*, many were doubtless real cases of violent seizure, without excuse even according to William's reading of the law. But this does not always follow, even when the language of the Survey would seem to imply it. Words implying violence, *per vim* and the like, are used in the legal language of all ages, where no force has been used, merely to mark a possession as illegal. We are startled at finding the Apostle Paul set down as one of the offenders; but the words "sanctus Paulus invasit" mean no more than that the canons of Saint Paul's church in London held lands to which the Commissioners held that they had no good title. It is these cases where one man held land which another claimed that gave opportunity for those personal details, stories, notices of tenures and customs, which make Domesday the most precious store of knowledge of the time.

One fruitful and instructive source of dispute comes from the way in which the lands in this or that district were commonly granted out. The incomer, commonly a foreigner, received all the lands which such and such a man, commonly a dispossessed Englishman, held in that shire or district.

The grantee stepped exactly into the place of the *antecessor*; he inherited all his rights and all his burthens. He inherited therewith any disputes as to the extent of the lands of the *antecessor* or as to the nature of his tenure. And new disputes arose in the process of transfer. One common source of dispute was when the former owner, besides lands which were strictly his own, held lands on lease, subject to a reversionary interest on the part of the Crown or the Church. The lease or sale—*emere* is the usual word—of Church lands for three lives to return to the Church at the end of the third life was very common. If the *antecessor* was himself the third life, the grantee, his *heir*, had no claim to the land; and in any case he could take in only with all its existing liabilities. But the grantee often took possession of the whole of the land held by the *antecessor*, as if it were all alike his own. A crowd of complaints followed from all manner of injured persons and bodies, great and small, French and English, lay and clerical. The Commissioners seem to have fairly heard all, and to have fairly reported all for the King to judge of. It is their care to do right to all men which has given us such strange glimpses of the inner life of an age which had none like it before or after.

The general Survey followed by the general homage might seem to mark William's work in England, his work as an English statesman, as done. He could hardly have had time to redress the many cases of wrong which the Survey laid before him; but he was able to wring yet another tax out of the nation according to his new and more certain register. He then, for the last time, crossed to Normandy with his new hoard. The Chronicler and other writers of the time dwell on the physical portents of these two years, the storms, the fires, the plagues, the sharp hunger, the deaths of famous men on both sides of the sea. Of the year 1087, the last year of the Conqueror, it needs the full strength of our ancient tongue to set forth the signs and wonders. The King had left England safe, peaceful, thoroughly bowed down under the yoke, cursing the ruler who taxed her and granted away her lands, yet half blessing him for the "good frith" that he made against the murderer, the robber, and the ravisher. But the land that he had won was neither to see his end nor to shelter his dust. One last gleam of success was, after so many reverses, to crown his arms; but it was success which was indeed unworthy of the Conqueror who had entered Exeter and Le Mans in peaceful triumph. And the death-blow was now to come to him who, after so many years of warfare, stooped at last for the first time to cruel and petty havoc without an object.

The border-land of France and Normandy, the French Vexin, the land of which Mantes is the capital, had always been disputed between kingdom and duchy. Border wars had been common; just at this time the inroads of the French commanders at Mantes are said to have been specially destructive. William not only demanded redress from the King, but called for the surrender of the whole Vexin. What followed is a familiar story. Philip makes a foolish jest on the bodily state of his great rival, unable just then to carry out his threats. "The King of the English lies in at Rouen; there will be a great show of candles at his churching." As at Alençon in his youth, so now, William, who could pass by real injuries, was stung to the uttermost by personal mockery. By the splendour of God, when he rose up again, he would light a hundred thousand candles at Philip's cost. He kept his word at the cost of Philip's subjects. The ballads of the day told how he went forth and gathered the fruits of autumn in the fields and orchards and vineyards of the enemy. But he did more than gather fruits; the candles of his churching were indeed lighted in the burning streets of Mantes. The picture of William the Great directing in person mere brutal havoc like this is strange even after the harrying of Northumberland and the making of the New Forest. Riding to and fro among the flames, bidding his men with glee to heap on the fuel, gladdened at the sight of burning houses and churches, a false step of his horse gave him his death-blow. Carried to Rouen, to the priory of Saint Gervase near the city, he lingered from August 15 to September 7, and then the reign and life of the Conqueror came to an end. Forsaken by his children, his body stripped and well nigh forgotten, the loyalty of one honest knight, Herlwin of Conteville, bears his body to his grave in his own church at Caen. His very grave is disputed—a dispossessed *antecessor* claims the ground as his own, and the dead body of the Conqueror has to wait while its last resting-place is bought with money. Into that resting-place force alone can thrust his bulky frame, and the rites of his burial are as wildly cut short as were the rites of his crowning. With much striving he had at last won his seven feet of ground; but he was not to keep it for ever. Religious warfare broke down his tomb and scattered his bones, save one treasured relic. Civil revolution swept away the one remaining fragment. And now, while we seek in vain beneath the open sky for the rifled tombs of Harold and of Waltheof, a stone beneath the vault of Saint Stephen's still tells us where the bones of William once lay but where they lie no longer.

There is no need to doubt the striking details of the death and burial of the Conqueror. We shrink from giving the same trust to the long tale of penitence which is put into the mouth of the dying King. He may, in that awful hour, have seen the wrong-doing of the last one-and-twenty years of his life; he hardly threw his repentance into the shape of a detailed autobiographical confession. But the more authentic sayings and doings of William's death-bed enable us to follow his course as an English statesman almost to his last moments. His end was one of devotion, of prayers and almsgiving, and of opening of the prison to them that were bound. All save one of his political prisoners, English and Norman, he willingly set free. Morkere and his companions from Ely, Walfnoth son of Godwine, hostage for Harold's faith, Wulf son of Harold and Ealdgyth, taken, we can hardly doubt, as a babe when Chester opened its gates to William, were all set free; some indeed were put in bonds again by the King's successor. But Ode William would not set free; he knew too well how many would suffer if he were again let loose upon the world. But love of kindred was still strong; at last he yielded, sorely against his will, to the prayers and pledges of his other brother. Ode went forth from his prison, again Bishop of Bayeux, soon again to be Earl of Kent, and soon to prove William's foresight by his deeds.

William's disposal of his dominions on his death-bed carries on his political history almost to his last breath. Robert, the banished rebel, might seem to have forfeited all claims to the succession. But the doctrine of hereditary right had strengthened during the sixty years of William's life. He is made to say that, though he foresees the wretchedness of any land over which Robert should be the ruler, still he cannot keep him out of the duchy of Normandy which is his birthright. Of England he will not dare to dispose; he leaves the decision to God, seemingly to Archbishop Lanfranc as the vicar of God. He will only say that his wish is for his son William to succeed him in his kingdom, and he prays Lanfranc to crown him king, if he deem such a course to be right. Such a message was a virtual nomination, and William the Red succeeded his father in England, but kept his crown only by the help of loyal Englishmen against Norman rebels. William Rufus, it must be remembered, still under the tutelage of his father and Lanfranc, had not yet shown his bad qualities; he was known as yet only as the dutiful son who fought for his father against the rebel Robert. By ancient English law, that strong preference which was all that any man could claim of right belonged beyond doubt to the youngest of William's sons, the English Ætheling Henry. He alone was born in the land; he alone was the son of a crowned King and his Lady. It is perhaps with a knowledge of what followed that William is made to bid his youngest son wait while his eldest go before him; that he left him landless, but master of a hoard of silver, there is no reason to doubt. English feeling, which welcomed Henry thirteen years later, would doubtless have gladly seen his immediate accession; but it might have been hard, in dividing William's dominions, to have shut out the second son in favour of the third. And in the scheme of events by which conquered England was to rise again, the reign of Rufus, at the moment the darkest time of all, had its appointed share.

That England could rise again, that she could rise with a new life, strengthened by her momentary overthrow, was before all things owing to the lucky destiny which, if she was to be conquered, gave her William the Great as her Conqueror. It is as it is in all human affairs. William himself could not have done all that he did, wittingly and unwittingly, unless circumstances had been favourable to him; but favourable circumstances would have been useless, unless there had been a man like William to take advantage of them. What he did, wittingly or unwittingly, he did by virtue of his special position, the position of a foreign conqueror veiling his conquest under a legal claim. The hour and the man were alike needed. The man in his own hour wrought a work, partly conscious, partly unconscious. The more clearly any man understands his conscious work, the more sure is that conscious work to lead to further results of which he dreams not. So it was with the Conqueror of England. His purpose was to win and to keep the kingdom of England, and to hand it on to those who should come after him more firmly united than it had ever been before. In this work his spirit of formal legality, his shrinking from needless change, stood him in good stead. He saw that as the kingdom of England could best be won by putting forth a legal claim to it, so it could best be kept by putting on the character of a legal ruler, and reigning as the successor of the old kings seeking the unity of the kingdom; he saw, from the example both of England and of other lands, the dangers which threatened that unity; he saw what measures were needed to preserve it in his own day, measures which have preserved it ever since. Here is a work, a conscious work, which entitles the foreign Conqueror to a place among English statesmen, and to a place in their highest rank. Further than this we cannot conceive William himself to have looked. All that was to come of his work in future ages was of necessity hidden from his eyes, no less than from the eyes of smaller men. He had assuredly no formal purpose to make England Norman; but still less had he any thought that the final outcome of his work would make England on one side more truly English than if he had never crossed the sea. In his ecclesiastical work he saw the future still less clearly. He designed to reform what he deemed abuses, to bring the English Church into closer conformity with the other Churches of the West; he assuredly never dreamed that the issue of his reform would be the strife between Henry and Thomas and the humiliation of John. His error was that of forgetting that he himself could wield powers, that he could hold forces in check, which would be too strong for those who should come after him. At his purposes with regard to the relations of England and Normandy it would be vain to guess. The mere leaving of kingdom and duchy to different sons would not necessarily imply that he designed a complete or lasting separation. But assuredly William did not foresee that England, dragged into wars with France as the ally of Normandy, would remain the lasting rival of France after Normandy had been swallowed up in the French kingdom. If rivalry between England and France had not come in this way, it would doubtless have come in some other way; but this is the way in which it did come about. As a result of the union of Normandy and England under one ruler, it was part of William's work, but a work of which William had no thought. So it was with the increased connexion of every kind between England and the continent of Europe which followed on William's coming. With one part of Europe indeed the connexion of England was lessened. For three centuries before William's coming, dealings in war and peace with the Scandinavian kingdoms had made up a large part of English history. Since the baffled enterprise of the holy Cnut, our dealings with that part of Europe have been of only secondary account.

But in our view of William as an English statesman, the main feature of all is that spirit of formal legality of which we have so often spoken. It: direct effects, partly designed, partly undesigned, have affected our whole history to this day. It was his policy to disguise the fact of conquest, to cause all the spoils of conquest to be held, in outward form, according to the ancient law of England. The fiction became a fact, and the fact greatly helped in the process of fusion between Normans and English. The conquering race could not keep itself distinct from the conquered, and the form which the fusion took was for the conquerors to be lost in the greater mass of the conquered. William founded no new state, no new nation, no new constitution; he simply kept what he found, with such modifications as his position made needful. But without any formal change in the nature of English kingship, his position enabled him to clothe the crown with a practical power such as it had never held before, to make his rule, in short, a virtual despotism. These two facts determined the later course of English history, and they determined it to the lasting good of the English nation. The conservative instincts of William allowed our national life and our national institutions to live on unbroken through his conquest. But it was before all things the despotism of William, his despotism under legal forms, which preserved our national institutions to all time. As a less discerning conqueror might have swept our ancient laws and liberties away, so under a series of native kings those laws and liberties might have died out, as they died out in so many continental lands. But the despotism of the crown called forth the national spirit in a conscious and antagonistic shape; it called forth that spirit in men of both races alike, and made Normans and English one people. The old institutions lived on, to be clothed with a fresh life, to be modified as changed circumstances might make needful. The despotism of the Norman kings, the peculiar character of that despotism, enabled the great revolution of the thirteenth century to take the forms, which it took, at once conservative and progressive. So it was when, more than four centuries after William's day, England again saw a despotism carried on under the forms of law. Henry the Eighth reigned as William had reigned; he did not reign like his brother despots on the continent; the forms of law and freedom lived on. In the seventeenth century therefore, as in the thirteenth, the forms stood ready to be again clothed with a new life, to supply the means for another revolution, again at once conservative and progressive. It has been remarked a thousand times that, while other nations have been driven to destroy and to rebuild the political fabric, in England we have never had to destroy and to rebuild, but have found it enough to repair, to enlarge, and to improve. This characteristic of English history is mainly owing to the events of the eleventh century, and owing above all to the personal agency of William. As far as mortal man can guide the course of things when he is gone, the course of our national history since William's day has been the result of William's character and of William's acts. Well may we restore to him the surname that men gave him in his own day. He may worthily take his place as William the Great alongside of Alexander, Constantine, and Charles. They may have wrought in some sort a greater work, because they had a wider stage to work it on. But no man ever wrought a greater and more abiding work on the stage that fortune gave him than he

"Qui dux Normannis, qui Caesar praefuit Anglis."

Stranger and conqueror, his deeds won him a right to a place on the roll of English statesmen, and no man that came after him has won a right to a higher place.